TO HIM BE PRAISE

TO HIM BE PRAISE

HYMNS TO CHRIST
IN THE FIRST MILLENNIUM OF THE CHURCH

Edited by
Costante Berselli

St Paul Publications

Original title: *Inni a Cristo nel primo millennio della Chiesa.*
Published in Italy by Edizioni Paoline. Copyright: Figlie di San
Paolo, Roma 1981.

Translated from the Italian by Sr Mary of Jesus O.D.C.

A selection of the hymns from this volume has been published under
the title of *Hymns to Christ,* illustrated with 50 miniatures.
Also available: *Sing the Joys of Mary.* Hymns from the first millennium of the Eastern and Western Churches.

St Paul Publications
Middlegreen, Slough SL3 6BT, England

English translation copyright © St Paul Publications 1982
First published in Great Britain May 1982
Printed by the Society of St Paul, Slough
ISBN 085439 211 4

*St Paul Publications is an activity of the priests and brothers of the
Society of St Paul who promote the christian message through the
mass media.*

CONTENTS

PREFACE

Written Christian history begins in the fourth century with the end of the persecution of Diocletian and the edict of tolerance promulgated in 313 at Milan, the capital of the Western Empire.

With this document the Emperor Constantine intended to give Christianity the possibility of a new strength of cohesion with the structures of the State, itself broken and weakened by an uninterrupted series of wars between the legions, quarrelling over the imperial elections.

After the promulgation of the edict, and with the Eastern provinces once more united under his rule, Constantine paid his attention to gaining the friendship of the Church hierarchy, and was specially watchful over the internal peace of the Church, disturbed by struggles with heresy.

When he perceived the danger of division inherent in the theories of the Libyan-Egyptian monk Arius, although a layman and not even as yet baptised, he did not delay to convoke the first ecumenical council at Nicea (Asia Minor), and showed the extent of his concern by placing the travelling carriages of the imperial court at the disposal of the Council Fathers for the journey. As honorary president, he presided over the Council, seated on a gilded throne, and by his programme of restoration, he endeavoured to prevent any division in the Church caused by internal discord.

Although Arius was condemned by the Council of Nicea, that was by no means the end of Arianism; it continued to spread with renewed vigour, causing no little difficulty within the Church and in the Church's relations with the imperial authority.

After the death of Constantine, and of two of the three sons between whom the empire had been divided, Constantius, the remaining son, found himself sole ruler of the

Roman Empire. While emperor in the West, probably from political calculation, he had embraced Arianism, hoping thereby to gain support from many accommodating bishops for his nascent caesarism.

The ascendency gained by the imperial power over the Church by the edict of 313 was used not to protect the Church but to dominate it and to force Arianism on to it by the strategy, among others, of placing Arian bishops in the most prestigious sees. In this way Auxentius became bishop of Milan.

To contest this Arian presence in the capital of the Western Empire, Hilary, bishop of Poitiers in France, intervened, though without success, to censure the relationship allowed by the hierarchy between Christianity and the government.

However, shortly before his death, at the instance of a group of discontented bishops whom he had tried to help while in exile in the East, Hilary returned to the West, and with unanswerable dialectic inveighed against "the illusion that would put human and earthly values before the will of God. O you bishops, who base your criteria on such concepts, what would have happened if the apostles had sought for political protection in their preaching of the Gospel? Did they not sing their hymns to God amid scourges and chains in prison rather than go begging for dignities at the imperial court? Now, instead, the protection of the powerful serves as a recommendation to faith in God; thus the mere fact that they go around boasting in the name of Christ presupposes that they are empty of all virtue on their own account . . . the ears of the masses are more holy than the hearts of their pastors who attribute divinity to Christ with their lips but empty their words of all content by their actions" (PL 10,605-618).

About ten years after this sharp diagnosis, in 374, Bishop Auxentius died in Milan; the Christian conscience of the people, who seemed to have accepted the government by the heretical bishop, was guided by a providential intuition to elect by popular acclamation the Consular Legate for Liguria and Emilia, whose seat was in Milan, as their bishop. Ambrose in the performance of his functions had gained the reputation at 35 or 37 of being an equable, but firm and resolute man.

Born in Treves in Germany, of a family of ancient Roman tradition, he was, at the time of his election, still a catechumen, with a sister, Marcellina, who had already received the veil of a virgin from Pope Liberius in Rome. He prepared for his mission by study, acquiring a profound knowledge of the scriptures and the Fathers, a preparation for pastoral activity in an epoch when paganism was no longer a live option. Intransigent against any return to the lingering vestiges of paganism, he showed great determination against the penetration of Arianism from the East.

When the Empress Justina tried to introduce an Arian bishop into a Milanese Church, Ambrose had the Basilica Portiana occupied by the faithful, who sustained a veritable and prolonged siege until the imperial court renounced its plan.

Together with this episode, the second half of the fourth century saw another great man, Augustine, bishop of Hippo (Bona, in Algeria).

Born at Tagaste, in northern Africa, he moved to Carthage to complete his classical studies and there took up the teaching of rhetoric (the art of writing and speaking). Leaving Carthage, he went first to Rome and then to Milan, still in the capacity of a teacher of rhetoric. In that city the preaching of Bishop Ambrose enlightened his spirit, tormented as it was not only by a way of life far from commendable but by the conflict between his philosophical ideas and the Christian truths taught him by his mother Monica and not entirely stifled in his spirit.

The enlightenment he received from Ambrose's discourses led him back to the faith of his adolescence and prepared him for baptism, which he received at the hands of Bishop Ambrose a year after the incident of the Basilica Portiana.

The two events, both decisive, the first in the life of a great bishop, the second by its opposition to the interference of the civil authority in the life of the Church

13

in this epoch, were recorded by Augustine in his *Confessions* (Book IX, Chapters VII and VIII).

Augustine writes that in the days immediately following his baptism, the echo of the hymns and canticles sung during the ceremony still filled him with emotion: "at the sound of such voices the truth sank into my soul with great sweetness" and "in the tears that flowed copiously, I found great contentment".

Augustine was aware that the singing of hymns had been introduced into the Milanese Church for the first time during the long siege sustained in the basilica, to prevent the faithful falling into weariness and melancholy, and "from that time, this practice, common in the Eastern Church, was diffused from Milan to almost all the Churches in the world". A milestone in the history of hymnody in the West.

This historical exordium, however brief, might appear redundant in an introduction to the hymns of the Church. On the contrary, it leads to the consideration of the fecundity of the Church's ancient hymns as revealed in the testimony of these two great figures of Western Christianity, who in equal measure worked to bring about that vast process of conceptual and disciplinary elaboration in the Church following on the death of Constantine. The two masters in relations between Christianity and empire found their apostolate strengthened by the singing and hearing of sacred hymns.

Pliny and Elder, the Latin writer of the first century after Christ and author of a Natural History in 37 volumes, when trying to describe the process whereby the branch of a tree endeavours to gain a favourable position in order to receive the sunlight it needs, to which botanists give the name of heliotropism, uses a concise Latin phrase: "Ramus edomatur, meditatione curvandi" — the branch exerts a determined and conscious effort to gain the desired position. In the same way, man curbs and prepares himself by persistent effort to transform willing into being, an effort in which meditation and contemplation concur, acting like the fire with which metal is tried.

Two of the great doctors of the Church in the second half of the 4th century, their spirits steeped in Christian truth, and their minds tempered by the study of philosophy, sacred scripture and the Apostolic Fathers, reconfirmed and proclaimed the singing of sacred hymns following in the traditions already laid down in the primitive Church. This consideration alone is sufficient to justify the present anthology of hymns.

THE HYMN IN LITURGICAL HISTORY

1. The hymn in the primordial cultual assembly. — 2. The historical roots of Christian hymnography. — 3. The area and the Fathers of hymnography in the first millennium.

The history of the earliest Christian times ends in the year 62 when Paul arrived as a prisoner in Rome, and was set down by Luke in the Acts of the Apostles.

After the Ascension the disciples left Mount Olivet and returned to Jerusalem where the first primitive nucleus of the Church was formed by a group of about 120 people. Peter, in his capacity as primate, proposed the election of another apostle to fill the place left empty by Judas.

The first group grew to about 3,000 baptised shortly after Peter's discourse on the day of Pentecost; these neophytes "were assiduous in attending the instruction of the apostles, the breaking of bread and the prayer" (Acts 2:42).

A great part of these first Christians, however, once the days assigned to the Jewish feast of Pentecost were over, returned to their cities and towns to take up again the rhythm of their everyday life; they had lived for some days in communion with the apostles and received from them the first teaching that gave life to the Christian community that flowered in that part of the world where the Jews of the diaspora were present, and who were the first to hear the Gospel preached.

1. *The hymn in the primordial cultual assembly*

As we read in the Acts of the Apostles, the cultic celebration consisted in a reunion where there were readings from the Bible with comments and teaching, the eucharistic function and the prayers.

Jesus had said at the Last Supper: "Do this in

memory of me", and so the first Christian communities repeated the ceremonial of the Last Supper.

The prayers recited during the eucharistic celebration, which specifically pertain to our topic, developed in the fullest acceptance of the term. We find testimony to this in passages in the Letters of St Paul: to the Ephesians (5:19): "when you are together sing hymns and psalms and spiritual canticles, singing to God in your hearts"; and to the Colossians (3:16): "Sing psalms, hymns and canticles to God in your hearts under the impulse of grace"; to the Corinthians (1 Cor 14:26): "When you have your meetings, let each one be ready with a psalm, or the gift of tongues or a canticle according to the inspiration of the Holy Spirit".

It is noteworthy that parts of the Letters themselves reveal in their expressions their origin in hymnic compositions heard, recalled or taught by Paul during his visit to the Church.

Such a text is to be found in chapter 2, verses 14-18, of the Letter to the Ephesians; and in chapter 1, verses 15-20, of the Letter to the Colossians. These verses contain a true Christological hymn, celebrating the primacy of Christ in the redemption: "He is the beginning, the first-born from the dead that in all things he may have the primacy. For it has pleased the Father that in him all fullness should dwell, and through him to reconcile all things to himself, making peace through the blood of his cross, through him, with all things in heaven . . ."

Also in the Letter to the Ephesians (5:14) we can recognise a strophe from an ancient baptismal or Easter hymn:

"Awake, you who sleep,
Arise from the dead.
Christ will shine upon you".

Substantially the Letters of St Paul make mention of two types of canticles which had become an integral part of the first liturgical assemblies:

17

1. The psalms; that is, the 150 psalms of the Davidic psalter, which the Church took over from the synagogue, both as regards their text and their melodic setting.

2. Spiritual canticles; texts taken from the Bible or improvised "under the inspiration of the Spirit", as Paul says; then transcribed and memorised.

The scheme of Mass as we see it in the book of Acts and the Letters of St Paul, and around which, bit by bit, with the insertion of hymnic prayer, the whole eucharistic liturgy developed (the word liturgy is used to indicate the order and the whole cultic ceremony), is described clearly for the first time by Justin — philosopher and martyr (c. 110-c. 165) — in his first apologia, addressed about the year 152 to the Emperor Antoninus Pius (138-161). Justin writes:

"On Sunday all who live in the city and the country come together in the same place. Then there is a reading from the Memories of the Apostles and the writings of the prophets. When the reading is finished, he who presides over the assembly takes up the word to exhort those present to live according to the teaching they have heard. Then all rise to their feet to offer prayer; then, after the bread, wine and water have been brought up to the president he himself offers prayer and thanksgiving to which they respond: Amen. At this point comes the breaking and distribution of the bread and wine to all those present, while it is sent by means of the deacons to those who cannot be there. Those who are rich and want to make an offering, offer what they wish; the collection is taken to the president who uses it to assist orphans and widows".

The ancient description of a Sunday Mass in the primitive Church is very suggestive and historically important. For our purpose, the most interesting phrases are: "all rise to their feet to offer prayer", and the president himself "offers prayer and thanksgiving" during and after the consecration of the bread and wine.

18

Justin, a pagan convert, born in Palestinian Syria, lived at Ephesus in Asia Minor and later spent two distinct periods in Rome; it can be presumed then that the description of the synaxis (a Greek term for the cultual assembly) corresponds with the liturgical norms of both East and West, not excluding Rome, at this time.

Coupling the phrase referring to the prayer and thanksgiving offered by the president as best he could with passages from the Pauline letters (where he recognises the charism of the faithful, that is, the supernatural gift of inspiration for the recital of hymns and prayers formulated personally) we can see how, within a single pattern, these hymnic prayers could differ according to person and place, in inspiration, construction and the customs reflected in them.

These differences would bring about in time the breakdown of liturgical unity; that would happen when prayers, hymns and canticles would be approved by the ecclesial authority and codified in liturgical formularies, that is, into a stabilised order for the celebration of rites.

The liturgy developed in different forms, owing to freedom as to formulae, the variety of local conditions, and the difficulty of maintaining stable and regular relations between the different Churches.

One point remained always stable: the hymns and canticles, read or chanted or recited in a cadenced prose under the form of prayer, continued to be the primary material from which the liturgy was formed.

The discourses and homilies, taking for their subject a hymn or prayer, are the charismatic recognition of the Fathers who pronounced them. The prayers of the martyrs were the best adapted to find a place in the eucharistic celebration, linking as they do the sacrifice of their life offered by the martyrs to the sacrifice of the cross.

The differing liturgies assumed in time well-defined forms which can be reduced to certain fundamental types:

— the Syriac type (with the sub-division of Antiochene, Jerusalem, Syro-Chaldean, Byzantine and Armenian);

— the Alexandrian type (dividing into Coptic and Byzantine);

— the Gallican type (including the Gallican, properly so-called, the Celtic and Mozarabic);

— the Roman type (with the one Roman rite and the one exception — substantially the ancient Roman rite — the Ambrosian of Milan).

The introductions to the individual hymns collected in this anthology include brief notices which illustrate the essential characteristics of the different liturgies.

As the proper character of each of these liturgies was gradually consolidated, the hymns, canticles and prayers in prose took the names of: tropari (texts giving solemnity to the liturgical celebration, having their place in the Divine Office and the Mass); anaphora (the central part of the Greek Mass); kondakion (poetic composition in the Byzantine Offices); preface (introductory chant to the central part of the Mass); antiphon (refrain evocative of the content of a psalm or canticle); etc.

This brief historical-liturgical preface is judged to be useful for an understanding of what guided the choice of compositions in this anthology, with its intention of representing hymnographical inspiration as manifested in different times and places.

2. The historical roots of Christian hymnography

Before proceeding with this brief introductory synthesis, it would be useful to define the meaning of three words. Our theme, in fact, calls for the use of three specific words: hymnography, the art of writing hymns and even collections of hymns, in particular those of religious import; hymnology, the study of sacred hymns; and finally, hymnody, the singing of hymns. It is useful to note also that the word "hymn" is given a wider meaning, to include not only compositions in verse but also in prose, destined for personal uplift, and chanted or proclaimed musically during a sacred function.

Justin's description of the Christian assembly was intended only to assure the emperor that the Christians were not committing any crime in their gatherings, still less plotting any conspiracy against the State.

Thus the lack of particulars regarding the prayer and thanksgiving that would have allowed us, after some eighteen centuries, to know the content of the texts and the musical characteristics of their settings.

Scholars in their study of liturgical history have sought to isolate from their context in the writings of the Fathers those passages that could constitute a hymn-prayer from the primordial liturgy. The musical characteristics of the accompaniment of these ancient texts is more easy to guess as we have an exact knowledge of the ancient musical instruments. The limited extension of their musical scale allows us to judge that the music which accompanied the chant in the primitive ecclesial assembly must have been gentle, almost monotone, not unlike the chants of primitive tribes who have not yet attained to modern culture. The sentiment with which the chant is expressed gives it its strength of penetration into the soul.

However, apart from the text and the music, the content of these hymnic prayers is of prime importance being always a profession of faith in the truths of Christianity. This is so much the case that they give testimony to a consolidated tradition which refutes and condemns any heretical propositions.

In proof of this we have Eusebius of Caesarea (c. 263–c. 310). In writing against the heresy of "dynastic monarchianism" aired at Rome by a certain Artemonus who, according to Eusebius, reduced "the Saviour to a simple man", the writer appealed to the "numerous psalms and canticles in which the brethren celebrated Christ, the Word of God, and recognised his divinity".

This quotation from Eusebius' *Ecclesiastical History* (V, 28, 5), apart from documenting the presence of heretical deviations even in the first centuries of the Church, is significant in revealing that even before the end of the persecutions, hymnography had become part of the

21

dialectic against schismatics, although it is not possible to establish that it was so used from the first.

It is certain, however, that the heretics used hymns to propagate their ideas and the Church was indirectly obliged to give a new form to her praises of God, in order to counter theirs.

The enrichment of hymnography stimulated by the doctrinal controversy began in the second century, with liturgical chants, doxological in character (that is, in glorification of the Blessed Trinity), as a help in opposing heretical attacks. They were lyrical compositions in prose rather than hymns, more like the psalms than poetry.

These innovations must necessarily have been spread over a long period of time; however, this long process of collecting together of texts for the progressive formation of the liturgy led up to the first decades of the fourth century when the Church obtained recognition and liberty from the emperor.

The new conditions attracted more of the cultured classes into the Church, people full of enthusiasm for free poetic creation; an enthusiasm, however, not unconnected with the reluctance on the part of intellectuals to accept biblical prose, which was considered poor, in place of classical reading; a reluctance which was quickly dispelled so that for the new converts the sacred scriptures would become a true discovery.

It was in this climate of religious and cultural ferment that the sacred hymns composed in rhythmic poetic style appeared, first of all in Syria with Ephrem (a brief biography precedes a selection of his hymns in this anthology), a celebrated and prolific poet whose works were all intended for liturgical use.

As we follow the line of events without stopping to analyse, which would be beyond the scope of this brief synthesis, we come to Hilary of Poitiers, who, returning from his exile in the East most probably brought back with him the West Syrian hymns which were quickly imitated.

We see, then, the connection with the episode of the siege in the Basilica Portiana, when Ambrose first introduced the singing of psalms and hymns into the Western Church, a fact to which Augustine testifies in his *Confessions*.

So it would be from the second half of the fourth century, after the Syrian and Greek hymnody, that one could speak of a Latin liturgical hymnody which developed rapidly in the ensuing centuries throughout Christian Europe.

3. *The area and the Fathers of hymnography in the first millennium*

In the preceding paragraphs we have noted the eminently doxological content of prayers and hymns, not excluding those originating from an individual charism, which the particular circumstances created by theological-doctrinal discussion imposed on the primitive Church.

When the Church was finally free to go out, across the borders of regions and continents, Christ the Redeemer, the centre of her missionary preaching, became also an essential element in her hymnography; not only for use in the liturgy itself but for use in individual and communitarian prayer as well. In other words, through the hymns, Christ was glorified by the learned and the poet who, enlightened by the new faith, strove to give a new face to their culture. In witness to this fact we have gathered into this anthology hymns composed by poets not yet Christian, or, being so, had not yet abandoned their form of expression which in vocabulary and expression remained close to classical pagan rhetoric.

The extra-liturgical hymn also came to be a means of uplifting reminder to the individual or community of the life of the Redeemer, from his birth to the public life, and above all a means of reliving the salient points of his passion, death, resurrection and ascension.

The hymn-prayer came to be used for the sanctification of the various times of the day and a plea for protection at the different hours of the Christian's day: morning, evening, night; to beg for forgiveness for one's own sins; to beg for future glory; in short, the hymn became the means of proclaiming the interior desire to live in conformity with the laws given by God to man and whose observance is only possible through the merits gained by Christ and offered by him to man.

If the hymn is all this, it is natural that in the course of time its development should have been parallel with the territorial expansion of the Church in the first millennium of her history.

This is first shown by the hymns from the ancient liturgies. The East, Asia Minor, Egypt and Africa are represented by the Armenian, Syriac, Coptic, Ethiopic and Byzantine liturgies (each has a brief introduction to the hymn chosen for this book); the West by the Ambrosian, Roman, Gallican and Mozarabic liturgies. Around the prayer expression officially codified in the various liturgies, there gathered a circlet of particular interpretations of hymnody, to each of which a short introduction is also given with the particular hymns; these are taken from the Collection of Alcuin, from the Gallican Formularies of Troyer and Paris, from the Bangor Antiphonary, and the Collection of Hiberno-Celtic Hymnography.

Rather in the background, in order to give greater prominence to the major figures, we have considered some small liturgical or paraliturgical collections such as the Scroll of Ravenna, the Euchology of Serapion, the Communion Chants, and a short series of Anonimous Hymns.

From the anonimous authors of the liturgy who belong to the natural evolution of time, we come to the Fathers of sacred hymnography, beginning with the martyrs, with Ignatius, Polycarp and Theodotus representing the East, and Genesius and Afra of Augusta the West. There is no need to list all the Fathers of whom the anthology gives at least one hymn. Arranged in order of date this anthology includes the most significant names; it opens in the East with Clement of Alexandria, the poet-theologian who presents Christ to us as the pedagogue, the teacher of the Christian, and closes with Simon the New Theologian, the mystic of the Byzantine Church considered to be the third theologian after John the Evangelist and John Damascene.

Turning from the East to the West, we have the figure of Ambrose who began liturgical chant in Europe. When Christianity, in spite of the repulse experienced, quickly came to terms with the culture of the succeeding centuries, this became an ineluctable component: there would be no lack of learned men to sing the faith in verse, such as Paulinus of Nola and Romanos called "the Melodious". Nor would there be lack of literary men, not yet sons of the Church but sensitive to the call of Christianity, like Claudius Claudianus; or those already converted to the faith but still influenced by classical and pagan texts, such as Ennodius of Pavia.

In the choice of hymns, made according to a plan to take in both the epochs and the territories where hymnography flourished, which fill the pages of this book, we can read both the history of the Church and the history of literature; but above all, this book is a text of Christian theology which offers a more solemn and convincing form to the prayer of a Christian.

C.B.

Costante Berselli was born in 1912. He completed his studies in the diocesan seminary in Mantua. As priest, he spent twenty years in the Curial Office, interrupted in the last year of the war by imprisonment for ten years, he has broadcast on Italian Radio.

THE GOSPEL OF LUKE

The Gospels contain two versions of the prayer taught by Jesus, that of Matthew (6:9–13) and that of Luke (11:2–4). Matthew's text, adopted by the Liturgy, is certainly closer to the Aramaic and Hebrew original; Luke's is all of a piece with his Gospel, written for the Gentiles (the people outside the Hebrew world, the pagans) and so some things that might seem too Semitic in character, such as the expression "who art in heaven" and the word "debt" which has been changed to "sin" (the Jews regarded sin as a debt due to God), have been omitted; it reveals, however, his preoccupation to search out the maximum clarity of thought. The brief formula appears to take into account Jesus' invitation to pray as he himself teaches; even to pray in secret, as in recollection everyone has the possibility to make his own aspirations. And so it seems fitting to open this anthology of hymnic prayers, the spiritual testimonies of men of differing times and in all weathers, with the prayer taught by Jesus as it is preserved for us by Luke.

1. Father;
   May your name be glorified;
   Your kingdom come;
   Give us day by day,
   The bread by which we live;
   Forgive us our sins;
   As we forgive those who have sinned against us;
   And do not allow us to be overcome by temptation.

IGNATIUS OF ANTIOCH

Ignatius, bishop of Antioch, called "Theophorus" (God-bearer), was taken to Rome and thrown to the wild beasts in the circus during the Trajan persecution (98–117). The persecution years are the only means we have for dating Ignatius. He was the first in importance among the Apostolic Fathers. He was a man of vigorous talent, animated by a lively faith in God and a mystic ardour. On his way to Rome, in chains, he wrote seven magnificent letters, anxious to guard the faithful against heresy and exhort them to maintain union with their bishop. Most notable, in fact, incomparable, is the Letter to the Romans from which we take this invocation pronounced by Ignatius when faced with the certainty of martyrdom.

2. Let no creature, visible or invisible, attract me, so that I may belong to Jesus Christ alone.

Fire and the cross; herds of wild beasts; torn, stretched, rent, lacerated limbs; dislocated bones; crushed body; and all the tremendous torments of the devil let them all come upon me if only I can rest in Jesus Christ.

All the kingdoms of this world and the joy of them are nothing to me. I prefer to die in Christ than to reign from one end of the earth to the other.

I seek him who died for us; I long for him who rose again for our sakes.

Be good to me, my brothers; do not impede my birth into life, do not kill me [by preventing me from dying for Christ], do not give to the world one who desires to belong only to God. Allow me to turn to that pure light: when I arrive there [in the arena] I will be a man of God indeed.

Let me imitate the passion of my God.

Let anyone who lives with God in his heart understand my desire, and sympathize with me in my torment.

POLYCARP OF SMYRNA

Polycarp (c. 70–c. 156), bishop of Smyrna, friend of Ignatius and teacher of Irenaeus of Lyons, was a disciple of the Apostle John. He was burnt to death as a martyr about the year 156, under the Emperor Antoninus Pius. The account of his martyrdom was set down shortly after his death by a certain Marcion, and is considered worthy of belief. They tied him to the stake. Tied thus, with his hands behind his back, Polycarp looked like a lamb chosen from the flock to be sacrificed. As the flames surrounded him, the martyr pronounced the following prayer; a solemn prayer, nourished by the scriptures, in which we can already hear the accents of the great doxology of the *Gloria*.

3. Lord, God almighty, Father of Jesus Christ, your blessed and beloved Son, who has taught us to know you.

God of the angels, of the whole of creation, of the whole race of the just who live in your presence: I bless you because you have judged me worthy of this day and of this hour; worthy to be added to the number of the martyrs; worthy to drink the chalice of your Christ, so as to rise up to eternal life in body and soul in the immortality of the Holy Spirit.

May I today be numbered among the martyrs in your presence as a precious and acceptable victim; bring to completion that which your will has prepared and revealed to me; God, faithful and true, for this grace and for all the others, I praise you, I glorify you, and bless you through our eternal heavenly priest, your beloved Son, Jesus Christ.

Through him, with him, and with the Holy Spirit, may you be glorified now and through all ages.

ACTS OF PETER

The Acts of Peter, a small book extant only in a mutilated form, was written by an unknown author between 180 and 190, in Syria or Palestine. It belongs, like the apocryphal gospels, to that vast literature imitating the New Testament, which abounded in the first centuries and which did not find a place among those the Church recognised to be inspired books.

The apocryphal texts, in fact, while containing a nucleus of historical material, have the tone of popular narrative, giving rein to fantasy in order to satisfy curiosity concerning particulars on which the sacred narrative maintains silence, and favouring dreams and visions such as were dear to a primitive community.

The Acts of Peter were translated into various languages; the incomplete Latin version is contained in the Acts of Vercelli, where the celebrated episode of Peter and Simon Magus is narrated.

We take the following prayer of the apostle to Christ from the Acts of Peter.

4. O Jesus, immaculate Lamb,
   you are both father and mother;
   my brother and my friend; . . .
   You are he who is all, and that all is in me;
   You are he who is, and nothing exists apart from you.

   Take refuge in him, you too, my brothers;
   and when you have understood that only in him will
   you have life,
   then you will receive that joy that was promised:
   "That which eye has not seen
   nor ear heard,
   nor has it entered into the heart of man to imagine".
   Grant to us, then, what has been promised.

   We praise you, we thank you, we bear witness to you;
   we, weak mortals, give you glory,
   you who alone are God, for there is no other.
   Glory to you, now and to the end of time.

CHALDEAN LITURGY

The Chaldean rite had its origin in Mesopotamia (now Iraq) but spread to the east, even as far as China. Today it is celebrated among the Nestorians of Kurdistan (the territory which divides Iran from Iraq), among Catholics in Iraq and Persia and among those who belong to the Malabar rite (India). The anaphora or offertory prayer which follows is a very ancient one, perhaps contemporary with that of Hippolytus of Rome. Its provenance seems to be Edessa (now the Turkish city of Urfi) from whence it passed into Syria where it still forms part of the eucharistic rite.

5. All creatures venerate and praise the adorable and glorious name of the most Holy Trinity, Father, Son and Holy Spirit, who in his goodness created the world and in his kindness saved men and granted eternal benefits to mortal men.

Thousands of heavenly spirits bless and adore you, myriads of angels with ardent spirits sing to your name. With the cherubim and seraphim they glorify and adore your grandeur, proclaiming ceaselessly, one to the other: Holy, holy, holy Lord of the universe; heaven and earth are full of your marvellous presence, of the splendour of your greatness. Hosanna in the highest heaven; hosanna to the Son of David! Blessed is he who comes and who will come with the power of heaven in the name of the Lord.

We announce your presence, Lord, we, your servants, who have received from you immense gifts, that we cannot repay.

You have put on our humanity, joining it to your divinity, you have raised our littleness on high, lifted us up from our prostration, given new life to our mortal flesh, pardoned our sins, remitted our debts; you have given light to our minds, overcome our enemies, brought honour to our poverty.

Lord, our God, our hymn of glory, gratitude and adoration echoes the superabundance of your grace, now and for ever and through all ages.

31

SYRIAC LITURGY

It is difficult to give any date to the Syriac prayer reproduced here, but it reveals the characteristics of a very ancient form along with sobriety on the titles given to the Virgin Mary. Christ the Saviour is invoked on the day of the nativity on behalf of the many needs of his people and in a broad vision of charity imploring present well-being and the future Good for one's neighbour. Its content and elegant style make it a prototype for the prayer of the faithful.

6. Jesus Christ, radiant centre of glory,
image of our God, the invisible Father,
revealer of his eternal designs,
prince of peace;
father of the world to come . . .

For our sake he took the likeness of a slave,
becoming flesh in the womb of the Virgin Mary,
without intervention of man;
for our sake, wrapped in swaddling bands and laid in
a manger,
adored by the shepherds and hymned by the angelic
powers, who sang:
Glory to God in the heavens
and on earth peace and good to men.

Make us worthy, Lord, to celebrate and to conclude in
peace the feast which magnifies the rising of your light,
by avoiding empty words, working with justice,
fleeing from the passions and raising up the spirit
above earthly goods
Bless your Church, formed long ago
to be united with yourself through your life-giving
blood.
Come to the aid of your faithful shepherds,

of the priests and the teachers of your Gospel.
Bless your faithful
whose only hope is in your mercy;
christian souls, the sick,
those who are tormented in spirit
and those who have asked us to pray for them.
Have pity, in your infinite clemency,
and preserve us in fitness to receive the future, endless
   good things.
We celebrate your glorious nativity
with the Father who sent you for our redemption,
with the life-giving Spirit,
now and for ever and through all ages.
Amen.

CLEMENT OF ALEXANDRIA

Titus Flavius Clement of Alexandria (b. ?–c. 215), an Athenian by birth but brought up in the culture of the Christian academy of Alexandria in Egypt, was a genial writer of prose who exercised a decisive influence on Christian literature by his teaching and masterly works (Origen was among his disciples). For these reasons he was considered to be the founder of a true and proper "theological science". The second part of a great work in three parts of an apologetic and pastoral character bears the title of *The Pedagogue*, a pedagogy of Christian morals in the following of Christ, the master of life, whose teaching should be received with docility. The hymn to Christ, the final end and norm of all things, from which we take two stanzas, closes the work.

7. Be propitious, O Father, Master, to your disciples;
   O Father, Guide of Israel, Father and Son who are
   one: Lord.
   Grant to those who obey your precepts,
   to be modelled in your image, and to enjoy,
   after they have been proved, the goodness of God
   and not the severity of his judgement.
   Grant that we may all live in your peace,
   that we may walk in the ways that lead to your city,
   resolutely passing over the waters of sin,
   sure of the guidance of the Holy Spirit,
   your ineffable wisdom.
   Grant that day and night, till our last hour,
   we may pray in thanksgiving and give thanks in prayer
   to the one Father and Son, the Son and the Father;
   the Son, the leader and master,
   together with the Holy Spirit.
   All belongs to the One, in whom is all.

Through him all is one, through him is eternity.
We are all his members; all ages are his glory.
To Goodness, to Beauty, to Wisdom,
To the Just One, all. To him be glory, now and for
all ages.

8. O Christ, Lord of the elect,
immortal Word of God the Father,
prince of wisdom;
strength in weariness;
joy without end;
Jesus, Saviour of the human race,
shepherd, protector, guide and moderator,
the heavenly pathway for the flock of the saints.
Fisher of men, you come to draw us out
from the sea of vice;
you draw out the fish that are saved from the menacing
   waves
and carry them along to the life of the blessed.
Guide us, shepherd of the human flock;
reign, O holy one, over the sons you have redeemed;
your steps, O Christ, are the road to heaven.
O eternal Word, infinite time,
immortal light, fount of mercy,
promoter of virtue, incomparable prize
of those who honour the Most High.

CYPRIAN OF CARTHAGE

Tascius Cecilius Cyprianus (beginning of the third century–258) was born of a rich pagan family of Carthage. A rhetorician before his conversion, within a short space of time after baptism he was ordained first priest and then bishop of the city; he governed the Church of Carthage during the Decian persecution, which became most fierce during the years 249–251. He was a prudent and energetic pastor, a defender of the faith and of the ecclesiastical discipline with regard to apostates and relations with the Church of Rome, but choosing moderate solutions and allowing charity to have the last word. His writing was always in the service of his pastoral duty, his the persuasive tone of one who loved to instruct. His works are read and utilised widely.

The meditative excerpt below is taken from the *Commentary on the Our Father*.

9. If Christ is the true sun and the true day,
    no hour should pass for the Christian
    without adoring his God;
    and so, we who are in Christ,
    that is, in the sun and true day,
    should spend the whole day in prayer;
    and when the sun draws nigh to its setting
    and night follows after,
    he who prays cannot fall into any evil;
    even then, in the night,
    there is light for the sons of light.
    How can we be without light
    when the light shines in our hearts?
    When can we be without sun
    if Christ himself is our sun?

HIPPOLYTUS OF ROME

Hippolytus of Rome (?–236) wrote his works in Greek, so they had a wider diffusion in the East than in the West. He is known as an exegete and a writer, and a pugnacious opponent of heresy. His character, however, puffed up by his polemics, was transformed into something of a libellist; through disciplinary questions inherent in his anti-heretical position, creating a kind of conventicle, he was opposed to the popes of the time to such a degree as to be considered the first anti-pope of history. Priest and then bishop, during the persecution of Maximinus Tracius (235–238) he was condemned to hard labour in the mines along with Pope Pontianus. After being reconciled, he died a martyr with him in the year 235 or 236.

Apart from the *Apostolic Tradition* from which we gain our knowledge of the ancient Roman liturgy, Hippolytus wrote exegetical, dogmatic and disciplinary tracts. His tract on the Pasch is certainly the inspiration for the paschal hymn which follows, even though it actually belongs to a later epoch.

10. It is the Pasch; the Pasch of the Lord . . .
O you, who are truly all in all! . . .
The joy, the honour, the food and the delight of every
     creature;
through you the shadows of death have fled away,
and life is given to all,
the gates of heaven are flung open.
God becomes man
and man is raised up to the likeness of God.

O divine Pasch! . . .
O Pasch, light of new splendour . . .
The lamps of our souls will no more burn out.
The flame of grace,
divine and spiritual,
burns in the body and soul,
nourished by the resurrection of Christ.

We beg you, O Christ, Lord God,
eternal king of the spiritual world,
stretch out your protecting hands
over your holy Church
and over your holy people;
defend them, keep them, preserve them . . .

Raise up your standard over us
and grant that we may sing with Moses
the song of victory,
for yours is the glory and the power for all eternity!
Amen.

THEODOTUS THE MARTYR

Theodotus came to Ancira (modern Ankara in Turkey) where he lived out his faith in charity, devoting himself to comforting the prisoners and martyrs and even attending to their burial. Accused by the ruler of the city during Diocletian's persecution, he was beheaded, after being tortured, about the year 304. He is commemorated in the martyrology on 18th May.

11. Lord, Christ Jesus, creator of heaven and earth,
   you do not abandon those who trust in you,
   I thank you for having found me worthy to be made
   a citizen of your heavenly city,
   a member of your kingdom.
   I thank you for having granted me to overcome
   the infernal dragon and crush its head.
   Give peace to your faithful
   and turn the persecution of your enemies upon me.
   Give peace to your Church
   and rescue her from slavery to the oppressor.

ORIGEN

Origen (Alexandria in Egypt 185–Tyre 253 or 254) is regarded as the greatest theologian of the Greek Church. His father Leonidas suffered martyrdom in the persecution of Septimius Severus (193–211) and Origen himself, in his old age, was tortured under Decius (249–251) but allowed to go free. Origen, by his intelligence, profound faith, mystical enthusiasm and culture, dominated the ecclesiastical, theological, apologetical, biblical and ascetic science of his time and is the greatest ecclesiastical writer of the epoch preceding Augustine. In him was united profane culture with a singular knowledge of scripture which he studied as textual critic and commentator, searching out the allegorical and spiritual meaning. Some of his homilies commenting on scripture end with an invocation, a turning to Christ, which is marked by a strongly personal note of affective piety.

We give here the prayer for pardon which ends the Fifth Homily on Isaiah.

12. Jesus, come, make yourself a servant for me.
Pour the water into the basin; come, wash my feet.
I know that what I ask is temerarious, but I fear your
    words:
"If I do not wash your feet, you can have no part with
    me".
Wash, then, my feet, that I may have a part with you.
But what do I say, wash my feet?
Peter could say this
for he needed only his feet to be washed
for he was all adamant.
But I, once bathed,
have need of that baptism
of which the Lord said:
"As for me, there is another baptism with which I
    must be baptised".

GENESIUS MARTYR

The only dates we possess are those of the persecution of Diocletian, during which Genesius was martyred, about the year 285. The city of Arles (France) considers him its glory, as Prudentius attests (Peristephanon 4, 35) and also Venantius Fortunatus (Carmina 8, 3, 157); his cult, however, was well known in even in Rome so much so that he was believed to be a Roman martyr converted to the faith — according to a legend without historical foundation — on the stage where he is said to have performed the art of mimeing. He was greatly venerated even at Milan; the Ambrosian liturgy accorded him a proper preface; a chapel was erected to him at the end of the fifth century, now the church of Saint Aquilino, close to the basilica of San Lorenzo in Milan.
We transcribe the prayer uttered while he suffered torture.

13. There is no other emperor, king or god,
apart from Christ Jesus . . . I believe in him alone,
him alone I adore, and am always ready
to die a thousand deaths for love of him.
No torment can drag from my heart my faith in him.
I repent of having derided the Christian faith
and the holy men who professed it
and of having been late in recognising and submitting
myself
to my true king and lord.

SERAPION OF THMUIS

At the end of last century, an important collection of prayers (Euchology) was found on Mount Athos. Two of these bear the name of Serapion who was abbot of the monastery of Thmuis in Lower Egypt from the year 339, and a friend of Athanasius. It has not been critically proved that the other prayers of the Euchology, thirty in all, are by the same Serapion. The Euchology represents a primitive liturgical collection of ancient Egypt and includes the prayer for the eucharistic celebration, for baptism, ordination, blessing of the oil of the sick, and a prayer for burial.

The prayer for the blessing of the people which we give here is notably relevant.

14. The hand of the only Son, alive and uncontaminated,
the hand which cures all our ills,
which sanctifies and protects,
is stretched out over the bowed heads of these people.
May the light of the Spirit,
the blessing of heaven,
the invocation of prophets and apostles
descend upon them.
May it keep their bodies pure in chastity,
their minds intent on study and the knowledge of the
mystery.
All in union, may they be blessed
through your only Son, Jesus Christ;
through him your glory and omnipotence is known
in the Holy Spirit,
now and for all ages.
Amen.

CYPRIAN OF ANTIOCH

We have no certain biographical knowledge of Cyprian of Antioch, of whom a legend says he was a magician before his conversion. Two prayers are wrongly attributed to him, taken, however, from the works of Cyprian of Carthage. They probably derive from the ancient baptismal liturgy and are intended to dispose the heart to penitence and a plea for pardon from God before receiving the sacrament. We give here an excerpt from one of the prayers.

15. I beg you, Son of the living God;
you have worked so many miracles;
you changed water into wine at Cana
to enlighten Israel;
you healed the eyes of the blind,
you restored hearing to deaf ears
and movement to paralysed limbs,
you corrected the stammering tongue,
freed the possessed,
made the lame run like the deer,
raised up the dead,
and taking him by the hand you made Peter
walk upon the water, safe from sinking.
You have left us this saying:
"Ask and you will receive,
knock and it will be opened to you.
All that you ask of the Father, in my name,
I too will ask of my Father, that you may have it".
I ask that I may receive, seek that I may find,
knock that it may be opened to me.
I ask in your name that you will ask your Father and
he will hear me.
I am ready to pour out my blood,
as a victim, for your name's sake,
to bear any torment.

You, Lord, are the one who hears and protects me;
defend me from the enemy.
May the angel of light protect me,
for you have said, "What you ask of me
with faith in prayer, I will grant". . .
May your Spirit work in me; your will be accomplished
   in me,
that I may be wholly yours,
all the days of my life.

LITURGY FOR THE EUCHARISTIC CELEBRATION

Apart from the liturgical collections which take us back to the 3rd century, we possess very few texts of the early popular and liturgical prayer. This is due to the ample freedom allowed to the celebrant in the spontaneous creation of prayer formulae (up to the end of the 5th century in the West, the 6th century in the East). However, certain prayers and canticles were soon entered, somewhat officially, in the liturgical books. This is the case with the evening prayer (see hymn 24). Scholars in this patristic sector are confident that other precious texts and fragments exist and will come to light. These were used as a profession of faith during communion. We propose four of them, dated 3rd–4th century.

16. Come now, with great joy,
you, the faithful, the new Israel,
come to the house of the Lord;
with hands that are purified
and solemn devotion
render him honour.

The creator of the universe
is once more mystically
immolated in the hands of the priest.
He who can not suffer in his divinity
has accepted suffering
in his humanity.

Before the eyes of his believers
there now takes place
an ineffable miracle . . .
The heavenly bread lies on the altar.
God who cannot be a victim
is sacrificed in this mystery;
the bread of heaven on the altar

nourishes, giving new life
to those who once were dead
through the guilty food
taken in Eden.

In the chalice flows the blood
which drained from his body
and is offered
by the hand of the priest
in the new holocaust;
the faithful drink of it
in expiation of their sins.

Never overcome,
as father he opens his heart
to the whole of humanity.

Let us be ready so as to be worthy
of him at his second coming;
may his Mother and the holy Apostles
intercede for us,
that his mercy
may gather us into the choir of all the saints.

17. May your sacrament, Lord Jesus Christ,
give us life
and the remission of sin:
the passion is offered on our behalf.
Gall you have drunk
to free us from all bitterness;

you have drunk the sour wine
to relieve our weariness.

You have been reviled
that the dews of immortality might inundate us;

you were beaten with scourges
that our weakness might be assured of eternal life;

you were crowned with thorns
that your faithful might be crowned
with the verdant laurels of love;

you were wrapped in a winding sheet
that we be reclothed in your strength;

you were laid in the tomb
that in the new age
we might receive a renewed blessing.

18. You, who once spoke to Moses
on mount Sinai,
have received from an immaculate Virgin
flesh that is free from all sin.

You who once pastured Israel,
now feed on the milk of a Mother
who has not known man.
O marvellous happening!

You who once punished kings
now save yourself from a king
by flight into Egypt.

You, seated in majesty [on a high throne]
were laid in a manger
retaining all your dignity.

And now, full of faith,
we praise the Mother and sing to the Son.
He who in heaven is God and has no mother,
has descended to earth and lived as though motherless.
To you be the glory!

19. We proclaim your death, Lord,
and sing, O Christ,
of your glorious resurrection.
We have been found worthy
to share in this mystical banquet.
Made glad by the spiritual gifts you offer
we sing with the angels
the song of victory.
Alleluia!

The Word dwelling in the Father's mind
is today placed on a cross;
by his own will
he is buried like any simple mortal;
but he is risen again on the third day;
and has brought to us the gift of his infinite mercy.

EUCHARISTIC CANTICLE

The canticle — eucharistic, paschal and reputedly eschato-
logical in content — certainly belongs to the primitive liturgical
collections; in fervent accents it invites the faithful to contemplate and adore the body and blood of Christ, the principle
of our salvation.

20. Today we have contemplated upon the altar
our Lord Jesus Christ . . .
Today we have heard his voice, powerful yet gentle,
admonishing us:
This is the Body which burns up the thorns of sin
and gives light to the souls of men . . .
This is the Body in whose presence
the daughter of the Canaanite was cured.
This is the Body, which, approached
in full confidence by the sinful woman,
set her free from the mire of sin.
This is the Body Thomas touched
and recognising, cried out:
my Lord and my God.
This is the Body, great and most high,
which is the principle of our salvation.

One day he who is the Word
and our Life determined
that his blood should be poured out for us
and offered for the forgiveness of our sins.
We have drunk of the blood
by which we have been redeemed,
restored, instructed, given light.
Who is entitled to celebrate the mystery of grace?
We have been found worthy to share in this gift.
Let us keep it to the end that we may hear
from his holy and blessed voice:

"Come, O blessed, to my Father,
Receive the inheritance of the kingdom prepared for
  you".

Then those who crucified the Lord will fear;
those who have not believed in the Father, Son,
and Holy Spirit will be ashamed;
those who have denied and not born witness to
the most holy Trinity, one God, will be lost.

As for us, beloved,
we celebrate the wonder of the baptism of Jesus,
his holy and life-giving resurrection,
through which salvation has come to the world.
We await the happy fulfilment of redemption
in the grace and love
of our Lord Jesus Christ,
to whom is due all glory, honour and adoration.

ANCIENT NATIVITY HYMN

This hymn derives most probably from an ancient liturgy for the Nativity, of Eastern origin, as is born out by the triple invocation to God as "Holy", peculiar to the prayers of the Eastern Church. The invocation applied to Christ is an explicit confession of his divinity.

21. Sons of men,
    do you truly speak of justice?
    Dwellers on the earth,
    do you truly judge with fairness?

We confess with unshakable faith
    that God, who was made man
    and who was given birth by a Virgin.
Before all time he was begotten
    of an immeasurable Father;
    now we adore him who became incarnate
    in a Virgin's womb.
He is the creator of all,
    himself remaining invisible and distinct from
      creation.
So we are able to say:
    in you, Lord, is clemency; glory be to you.
O holy God,
    you have deigned to be born, a tiny child, from
      a Virgin.
O God, holy and strong,
    you have willed to rest in the arms of Mary.
O God, holy and immortal,
    you have come to rescue Adam from hell.
O immaculate Virgin, Mother of God, full of grace,
    Emmanuel, whom you have carried,
    is the fruit of your womb.
In your maternal bosom you have nourished all men.

You are above all praise and all glory.
Hail, Mother of God, joy of the angels.
The fullness of your grace
goes beyond what the prophets foretold.
The Lord is with you,
you have given birth
to the Saviour of the world.

EASTER HYMN

The hymn, which is presumed to date back to the 3rd–4th century, is an acrostic on a fly-leaf, with six strophes each of four lines followed by a refrain. It is preserved in a 6th century papyrus from which the first strophe is certainly missing. It exalts Christ, born of the Holy Spirit and of the Virgin Mary, as the new Moses who saves lost people.

22. We glorify you, O Christ, singing: glory to the Lord!
He was born of the Holy Spirit in order to give us life.
He deigned to dwell among us.
To him we render our veneration,
crying out together: glory to the Lord!

Behold: the Virgin has given birth to Emmanuel.
He has come down from heaven,
has saved from Egypt a people that was lost.
Let us exalt him, crying: glory to the Lord!

He has willed to overcome our enemy;
has made his dwelling in the Virgin Mary:
the invisible has become visible in flesh.
Let us adore him, crying out: glory to the Lord!

Born of a woman ever virgin,
the Word of truth rose again for us.
Let us celebrate the Lord,
intoning: glory to the Lord!

Light from light, Christ our king
is risen for us.
He has saved us from the land of Egypt;
all together let us sing: glory to the Lord!

ANONYMOUS HYMN TO CHRIST
THE ONLY-BEGOTTEN

This prayer-hymn seems to be a paraphrase of the first chapter of Paul's Letter to the Colossians in which he exalts Christ as Lord of the universe and of history. The text, mutilated, is found in a papyrus preserved in the collection of the Archduke Ranieri at Vienna. The numerous repetitions have been eliminated to make the meaning clearer.

23. The stars that shine
and the powers in motion
all vanish
in the splendour of your light
and remain still
before the power of your greatness.
You alone are visible, you reveal
the image of the Father almighty,
and thus you manifest
the sublimity of the Father and the Son.
As the Father is almighty in the heavenly sphere,
so are you, the Son, in our universe
the first born, the guide and lord of all power;
you, from the beginning, are the second grandeur
that comes from that of the Father;
you are the foundation of all the world.
You are our archetype,
the mind which ordains and the one who steers;
you are the way and the door
that opens into light.
You are the image of justice;
you are ever our shining star.
To you we render thanks, praise and blessing.
Before you we bend the knee
and we ask, with trust, that we be made holy.

Grant that we may be ever strong in faith,
sound in mind and body
to sing for ever and without ceasing your praises,
that you, the Immortal, the Infinite, the Eternal
may be celebrated in every place.
You are the model and essence of the Spirit,
you are our blessed Father,
our king and our God.
With eyes fixed on you,
we shall not die, O Lord;
if we confess your name,
we shall not be lost.

ANCIENT EVENING HYMN

This hymn, still recited in the Evening Office of the Greek Church, seems to belong to an earlier date than the *Gloria* (the oldest codex containing the *Gloria*, the Codex Alexandrinus, dates back to the 5th century). Basil writes about this hymn in his tract on the Holy Spirit (29, 33): "Our fathers did not wish to receive the grace of the evening light in silence; as soon as it appeared, they blessed God. We do not know the name of the author of this hymn of thanksgiving, an ancient canticle which all the people continue to recite". The hymn presumably dates back to the 3rd–4th century.

24. O Christ Jesus, radiant light
of the immortal glory of the Father of heaven!
As the sun sinks to its setting
we are face to face with the twilight of evening:
we honour God, Father, Son and Holy Spirit.
You are worthy ever to be hymned by voices that are
pure,
Son of God who gives us life.
The universe proclaims your glory.

PRAYER FROM AN EPIGRAPH

Many expressions of faith of the first Christian generations have come down to us in the form of an epigraph, which preserves in a personal and perhaps spontaneous form an ancient mode of prayer. These inscriptions on stone, belonging not to literature but to life, witness to faith in the Most Holy Trinity, in Christ and in the Holy Spirit. They are an auspicious prayer for the life above and beg for intercession with God. Placed on the tombs of the dead, these epigraphs were multiplied above all from the end of the 4th century, after the close of the persecutions. The greater number has been found in Egypt. The prayer in the form of a litany addressed to Christ, which we give here, in which there are evident references to primitive liturgical hymns, is carved on a sarcophagus found in a necropolis at Djebel Riha, between Aleppo and Alexandretta.

25. He who is immortal has suffered much for us.
Come to help us, Son of God, born of Mary!
Christ Jesus, come to our aid, born of Mary!

Heavenly shoot from the stock of David,
come to our aid, O Son, born of Mary!
Christ Jesus, come to our aid, O Son, born of Mary!

May the one immortal Son be praised over all the
earth.
Come to our aid, O Son, born of Mary!
Christ Jesus, come to our aid, O Son, born of Mary!

In your clemency you came from heaven to earth.
Come to our aid, O Son, born of Mary!
Christ Jesus, come to our aid, O Son, born of Mary!

Master of true life from all eternity.
Come to our aid, O Son, born of Mary!
Christ Jesus, come to our aid, O Son, born of Mary!

COPTIC LITURGY

The ancient Church of Egypt, later known as "Coptic" (i.e., Egyptian), numbers among its sons men of such spiritual calibre as Athanasius and Cyril; and it has the great merit of having kept alive and fervent even in Islamic surroundings, always hostile and often oppressive, for more than twelve centuries (from 640 to the beginning of the 19th century). Its liturgy, going back to the tradition of early Egyptian Christianity, is simpler in rite than others of the Eastern Churches. There are three forms: that most in use is that of Basil, the least used is that under the name of Cyril, and that of Gregory is reserved for solemnities.

We give here the universal prayer to Christ from the anaphora taken from the liturgy of Gregory.

26. O Christ, our God, we beg you:
give stability and strength to the Church,
implant in the depths of our souls
the harmony of love,
that the integrity of faith may grow.
Give firmness to the shepherds
and soundness to the flock.
May the clergy be irreprehensible in their morals,
the monks continent,
the virgins pure,
married couples in accord;
may the penitent receive your pardon;
the rich be generous,
those in power, moderate;
may the poor receive help.
Be strength to the old
and teacher to the young.
Enlighten those without faith,
make divisions in the Church to cease,
break the pride of heretics
and deign to hold all united
in concord and love.

ETHIOPIC LITURGY

The rite or liturgy of Ethiopia grew under the influence of the Coptic or Alexandrian-Egyptian rite, from which were chosen texts to be translated from the Greek. However the language in which the Ethiopic liturgy is celebrated is that of the kingdom of Aksum on the Tigris. Even when Aksum ceased to be the capital of the Abyssinian state, it remained the holy city where the kings were crowned. Splendid obelisks came to light among its ruins, one of which, 24 metres high, was taken to Rome in 1937 and erected near the Circus Maximus. The rite, bound up with the ancient language, remained almost unknown and little studied, especially in what referred to song and music, and bore no relation to other Christian liturgies. The Ethiopic rite possesses a rich patrimony of very ancient liturgical hymns such as the one reproduced here which seems to belong to the 4th or 5th century.

27. Holy Lord, Holy one, strong,
    living and immortal,
    son of the Virgin Mary,
    have mercy on us!

    Holy Lord, Holy one, strong,
    living and immortal,
    baptised in the Jordan and raised up on the cross,
    have mercy on us!

    Holy Lord, Holy one, strong,
    living and immortal,
    who rose from the dead on the third day,
    and having ascended into heaven sit at the right hand
      of the Father
    and will come again in glory
    to judge the living and the dead,
    have mercy on us!

Glory be to the Father and to the Son and to the Holy
   Spirit
now and for ever through all ages.
Amen! So be it!
Holy Lord, living Trinity;
have mercy on us!

AFRA OF AUGUSTA

We know little of the life of this young woman. According to her "passion" she was a public sinner. She was arrested while still a catechumen at the height of the Diocletian persecution, probably in the year 304. Condemned to the fire, she was burnt on a small island in the middle of a river running close to Augsburg (in Latin: Augusta) in federal Germany. From the midst of the flames her voice was heard giving thanks to Jesus Christ with the prayer which we here transcribe.

28. Lord, God almighty, Jesus Christ, who came to call not the just but sinners to repentance, in fulfilment of your promise you have graciously said: In the moment that the sinner repents of his fault, I forget his sin.

Accept my repentance in this hour of pain, and by means of this fire prepared for my body, set me free from the eternal fire that would burn both soul and body.

I thank you, Lord Jesus Christ, for having accepted me as a holocaust to your name. I thank you for having offered yourself on the cross as a victim for the whole world; you, the just for the unjust; the good for the evil; you, the innocent, a victim for sinners.

I offer my sacrifice to you, who with the Father and the holy Spirit, live and reign, God, for ever and ever. Amen!

EPHREM SYRUS

Ephrem is the most eminent among the Syrian writers of the 4th and 5th centuries. Born at Nisibis in 306 (modern Nisaybin, in south-east Turkey) of a Christian family, he studied and taught in the city until it was conquered by the Persians in 363. He then moved to Edessa, in the Roman province of Syria, where he founded "the Persian school", so called because it was frequented by many Christians of Persian origin. There he taught until his death in 373. Of a contemplative soul, Ephrem gained from his studies and contacts with God a knowledge of the divine mysteries of which he sings in his works. His immense theological and poetical productivity earned him the title of "lyre of the Holy Spirit"; in fact, he exalts the beauty of faith in order to defend orthodoxy, and he instructs the faithful with his songs. His most sincere poetry is found in the *Songs of Nisibis,* a composition basically historical in which he narrates his country's misfortune during the Persian wars. His poetic works were soon translated by the Greeks who were rather poor in Christian poetry; and later had much influence on the Byzantine liturgy.

29. On this day the new bread of the spirit
has gone up to heaven.
The mysteries were revealed in your Body
which has gone up as an offering.
Blessed be your bread, O Lord!

The Lamb has come to us from the house of David;
the priest, from the stock of Abraham,
has become for our sakes the Lamb of God,
the new minister of sacrifice.

His body is the victim, his blood is our drink.
Blessed be the new sacrifice!

He has descended from heaven like the light;
is born of Mary as a divine shoot;

as a fruit he has fallen from the cross;
and is offered up to heaven as the first fruits.
Blessed be his will!

You are the offering of heaven and of earth,
immolated and at the same time adored.
You came to be a victim,
you ascended as a singular offering
you ascended Lord,
bearing with you the offering of your sacrifice.

30. Lord, Christ Jesus, king of kings, you have power over life and death; you know the intimate secrets and none of our thoughts and sentiments are unknown to you. Repair the evil which I have done in your sight.

My life declines from day to day and my sin is growing. O Lord, God of soul and body, you know the extreme frailty of my soul and of my flesh, give strength to my weakness and sustain me in my anguish.

You, who are my powerful support, know that I am esteemed by many. Give me a grateful heart, which will not forget your benefits, Lord of infinite goodness! Forget my many sins and pardon all my treachery.

Lord, do not despise the prayer of one who is sorry; keep me in your grace as you have kept me in the past. This has shown me the wisdom of: blessed are those who pass swiftly through life, for they will receive a crown of glory.

Lord, I praise and glorify you in spite of my unworthiness, for your mercy to me has been without limit. You are my help and my protector. May your name be ever praised!

To you, O Lord our God, be glory!

31. I fall in adoration at your feet, Lord!
I thank you, God of goodness;
God of holiness, I invoke you,
on my knees, in your sight . . .

For me, an unworthy sinner,
you have willed to undergo the death of the cross,
setting me free from the bonds of evil.

What shall I offer you in return for your generosity?

Glory to you, friend of men!
Glory to you, most merciful!
Glory to you, most patient!
Glory to you who forgive sin!
Glory to you who have come to save us!
Glory to you who have been made man
 in the womb of a Virgin!
Glory to you who have been bound!
Glory to you who have been scourged!
Glory to you who have been derided!
Glory to you who have been nailed to the cross!
Glory to you, laid in the sepulchre, but risen again!
Glory to you who have preached the Gospel to men
 and have been believed!
Glory to you who have ascended to heaven!
Glory to you, seated at the right hand of the Father
 and who will return with him, in majesty, among
  the angels,
  to judge those who have disregarded your passion!

The powers of heaven will be shaken;
all the angels and archangels, the cherubim and
 seraphim
will appear in fear and trembling before your glory;
the foundations of the earth will quake
and all that has life will cry out before your majesty.
In that hour let your hand draw me beneath your
 wings,
and save me from the terrible fire, from the gnashing of
 teeth,
from the outer darkness and from despair without end.

That I may sing to your glory:
glory to him who through his merciful goodness
has deigned to redeem the sinner.

32. O victim not destined for the sacrificial fire,
receive my prayer
as a holocaust, and accept my invocation;
let my tears be the blood of a victim of expiation
and be accepted by you on festive celebrations.
My sublime saviour, welcome my offerings
full of love, and grant my prayer,
as I wait anxiously, O my master,
to know that it is accepted.
You received in your side the thrust of the lance
and showed me all your love
in your passion suffered for me;
you have saved me and welcomed me into your house:
with your balm
you have soothed my pain;
with your bread you restored me;
and I lived happy and secure
in your dwelling place.

33. Your presence brings courage;
sweet is your exhalation
and venerable your face,
O holy God.
Every form of life springs from you,
you are the bread of life in the house of bread
    [Bethlehem]
because you have life from the only source of life;
your breath draws us gently,
full of wisdom is your infancy;
you will be desired as food, O beneficent
heavenly nourishment . . .

O Son of God, you came to reunite the holy flock;
shoot from the Virgin, you became the lamb;
having heard your voice calling her

ε

the lost sheep ran to meet you.
O lamb who brought holiness into the world;
O little child and yet ancient of days,
O shepherd and yet a young lamb
benign and affable!

34. Blessed are you, O night, the last, which completed
the night of the exodus from Egypt; celebrating this
minor pasch, our Lord made himself the great pasch;
one pasch inserted in the other, a feast in a feast.
Behold the passover which passes away and that which
does not pass; one prefigures, the other is accomplishment.

Blessed are you, O holy place, where our Lord broke
the bread that had become his body. The narrow
refuge opened out to the whole world, which was
entirely conquered by it; with Moses there came
from the glorious mountain top a covenant to last but
a short time; from this modest abode, instead, there
came a pact of extraordinary greatness that changed
the whole world.

The exploits of Moses were only prefigurative, weak in
themselves. It was opportune, therefore, that they
should have more consistency so as not to be forgotten
before what they prefigured came to pass. On the
other hand it was opportune that the greatness of our
saviour should be hidden, for the natural glory of
God may not be seen by any creature save under the
appearance of frail human flesh.

O blessed room! Which, though narrow, stands before
the whole world; what was done in you this night,
though so little, fills the entire universe! O blessed
supper room, in which bread was broken by consecrated hands. Within your walls was crushed into
the chalice of salvation the little cluster of grapes
born of Mary.

O happy place! Nothing has ever happened or will ever happen like to what you have seen: the Lord, made altar of sacrifice, priest, bread, chalice of salvation. He alone is enough for all; and no-one is necessary to him; he is the altar and the lamb, the victim and the one who sacrifices, the priest and the spark for the fire.

O happy supper room! Never was feast been prepared such as that which was prepared in you: not in the palaces of kings, nor in the holy ark, nor in the holy of holies of the temple. Within your walls the bread was broken, by the first-fruits; you were the first Church of Christ; within your walls was seen the first of all oblations.

GREGORY NAZIANZEN

Gregory (c. 330–389) was born in Nazianz in Cappadocia (the region in the east of Asia Minor belonging to Turkey) and was ordained at about the age of thirty by a tyrannical act of his father. Later, having become a bishop, he resigned his see almost at once, being bewildered by intrigues and complications of a practical character. Being drawn rather to meditation and the literary life than to action, he is known among the Greeks as the "theologian" or the "Christian Demosthenes" and his introverted and dissatisfied spirit is apparent in his homilies, discourses and poetry. With Basil and Gregory of Nyssa he formed a triad of luminaries of Cappadocia. From the doctrinal point of view the best part of his writings is contained in 45 discourses, among which those in defence of the doctrine of the Trinity are the most notable. 245 letters have also come down to us, together with some poems. His personal vicissitudes and acute sensibility give a special tone to Gregory's writings.

35. O Pasch, great and holy mystery that purifies the
universe,
I would speak to you as if you had a soul.
O Word of God, light and life, wisdom and power!
I greet you with your many names.
Illustrious shoot, breath and image of the Spirit!
O Word of God, visible being in whom all is assumed
and all governed by your power!
Deign to listen to my words:
they are not the beginning
but certainly the fulfilment of my offering.
Grant that they may be both thanksgiving and
supplication.
Grant that I may bear only the trials of the spirit
that bring the reward assigned to our life.
Lighten the weight of the body;
You know, O Lord, how heavily it weighs.

Mitigate the severity of your judgment,
when we come to be winnowed by you.
But if our desires will be realised
grant that we may set out on our way and find
    welcome
in the heavenly mansions.
We will go on offering to you an acceptable sacrifice,
on your altar, Father, Word and Holy Spirit.
To you be the glory, the honour and the power
    through all ages.
Amen.

36. Christ, Word of God,
light of light, without beginning,
help of the Spirit, we praise you.
Threefold light of one undivided glory,
we praise you.

You have banished the darkness and created the light
and in this you have created all things.
To matter you have given life
giving it the imprint of the face of the world
and the traits of its beauty.

You have illumined man's Spirit
with reason and wisdom.
Your eternal light is reflected everywhere,
so that, in the light, man might discover
true beauty, and all become luminous.

You have lit up the heavens with variegated lights.
The night and the day you have commanded to take
    turns
in a rule of fraternal friendship;
the first brings to an end the fatigue of the body,
the other spurs us on to work as commanded;
and we flee from the darkness
to hasten towards that day
which no sadness of the night
can ever bring to an end.

Give to my eyelids a light slumber
that my voice may not long remain silent.
While created things watch to sing psalms with
  the angels,
may my sleep be ever restful in your presence;
may the night make me oblivious of the day's sins,
and its oddities not beset my dreams.

37. Give me strength, O Christ. Your servant is undone.
My voice, singing to you, is now silent. How can you
  allow it?
Give me strength, and do not abandon your minister.
I would have health once more;
sing to your praise and sanctify your people.
I beg you, my strength, do not desert me.
If my faith has grown less in the storm
Yet I would return to you.

38. If I were not yours, my Christ,
I would feel a finite creature,
I have been born and my life is dissolving away,
I eat, sleep, rest and walk,
sicken and am healed;
numberless are the desires and torments that assail me.
I enjoy the sunlight and the fruit of the earth;
but I die and my flesh will crumble into dust,
like that of the animals who have not sinned.
What more have I than they?
Nothing more, if not God.
If I were not yours, my Christ,
I would feel a dead creature.

39. Immortal sovereign, you are the great God, and as
your judgment is absolutely just you will come to
judge me: how, then, can I look upon you, O Word?

How can I fix my gaze on your throne, after I have made myself unworthy of heaven and earth and all creation? The tempter seized me and flung me into the depth of hell, into the immense abyss; the seducer, violently giving chase, has captured me and flung me into the deepest darkness of hell.

Have pity on me, O God, reach out your hand to me, raise me up . . .

Redeemer, we pray to you; unhappily we have committed injustice in body, soul and mind: we have sinned against you and have often broken your law . . .

We acknowledge our faults; do not look with anger upon us . . .

Have compassion on me, O Saviour, and do not allow me to be lost through my faults. I am, in fact, your son and the son of your handmaid. Besides, O Word, for my sake you have suffered a fearful death.

HILARY OF POITIERS

Hilary (310/320–368) was born in Poitiers in France of an illustrious pagan family and received an excellent education. He received baptism late, and although married by then, was elected bishop of the city about the year 350. Brilliantly talented as a theologian, and an able dialectician, he was tenacious in his opposition to Arianism, and so became inimical to the Emperor Constantius who, in 356, banished him to Phrygia (Asia Minor). From there, Hilary continued to defend orthodoxy, entering into contact with Eastern theology and studying doctrine. Leaving Phrygia, he returned to France, to his episcopal see, where he continued in his enlightened opposition to the Arian heresy.

His works reveal a depth of thought in which reason and faith each have their part. Some hymns, although somewhat obscure and contorted, are the first solitary beginnings of the period of Latin hymnography. The hymn that follows is not considered to be his, but its attribution to Hilary is a positive note in favour of this text.

40. O resplendent giver of light,
    like lightning at your command
    the time of darkness is past
    and daylight, regiven, spreads abroad.

    You are the true giver of light to the world,
    not as the tiny star,
    which, harbinger of the sun's rising,
    burns only with a feeble flame;

    but brighter than the fullest sun,
    all light and day,
    you light up the deepest sentiments
    of our hearts.

Assist us, O Creator of the world,
mirror of the light of the Father,
for our flesh
is fearful of losing your grace.

And full of your Spirit
having our God with us
may we not fall a prey
to the deceits of the treacherous tempter.

So that working in the world,
according to the needs imposed by our life,
far from any stain of sin
we may live according to your laws.

May chastity of mind
overcome the shameful passions of the flesh,
may the spirit preserve in holiness
the temple of a body that is chastened.

This is the hope of the soul in prayer,
these the vows which we offer:
that the light of the morning
may persist even during the night.

Glory to you, O Lord,
glory to the Only-begotten
with the Paraclete Spirit
now and for all ages.

AMBROSE

Ambrose (c. 339–397) was probably born in Treves (West Germany) and studied rhetoric and jurisprudence. About the year 370 he became Consular Legate of Emilia and Liguria with his seat at Milan, the capital of the Western Empire. In 374, while still a catechumen, he was proclaimed bishop of Milan by the unanimous voice of the clergy and people. He is considered the father of sacred hymnody in the West, having been the first to introduce the singing of hymns into the liturgy, some of his own composition. Following on him there was a flowering of hymns, which, being similar in metre and structure to those of Ambrose, are generically termed Ambrosian. However not all those that come down to us under his name are his work, and it is not possible to be certain of which, among these numerous hymns, is undoubtedly written by Ambrose. Augustine testifies to the authenticity of four hymns, among which is the Matins hymn "Aeterna rerum conditor" (Retractiones, 1, 21) which we give here.

41. O eternal maker of the world,
who rules over night and day
dividing up our daily round
to ease the body's weariness.

O night light for wayfarers
Which distinguishes night from night,
the dawn bird now sings aloud
calling up the light of the sun.

Lucifer [day star], unveiled by him,
drives darkness from the face of heaven
and malefactors in their troops
abandon now their brigandage.

Sailors gain strength as he appears,
and the sea's waves grow calm again;
hearing him, the Rock of the Church
[Peter] weeping, mourns his sin.

74

Let us arise then speedily.
The cock awakens those who sleep
and rouses up the drowsy ones;
the perjurors are accused by him.

At cock crow hope is born again,
and health returns to those who ail;
the brigand hides his dagger now,
and faith revives in apostate soul.

Jesus, look on those who waver;
and, looking, help us to be firm;
under your care shame fades away
and tears wipe out the stain of sin.

O light, shine now within our souls
and torpor fly from every mind;
and at the dawn our voices rise
in songs of prayer and praise to you.

42. Christ, our Redeemer,
begotten of the Father, the Father's only Son,
the only ineffable birth
before time began.

You, the light, the splendour of the Father,
you, the everlasting hope of all,
hear the prayer that from your faithful people
rises to you from every corner of the earth.

Remember, O Saviour, that in time,
being born from a spotless Virgin,
you have assumed our human nature.

The heavens and the earth,
the sea and all that is in them
glorify you this day
with a canticle of joy,
for it is the day that saw your coming.
We, too, who have been redeemed
in your blessed blood,
remembering your birth
raise up a new canticle.

43. Splendour of the Father's glory,
spreading the brightness of true light,
ray of light, fount of every splendour;
you, the day that lights up every day.

You, the true sun, enter in
beaming with a steady light
implanting deep within our senses
the flame of the Holy Spirit.

In our prayer we invoke the Father too,
Father of eternal glory;
the Father of all powerful grace
drive far from us the treachery of neglect.

Inspire in us strong action,
break the teeth of the evil one,
make easy that which is difficult,
give us grace to work always with wisdom.

Guide and sustain our mind
in a body that is healthy and reverent;
may faith burn ardently with love,
free from malice and deceit.

Christ be to us our food,
and faith for us be drink;
happily may we taste
the sober inebriation of the Spirit.

May this day pass in joy;
with modesty like the dawn,
faith burn bright as midday;
and mind know no evening at all.

The dawn proceeds in its course;
the Son is wholly our dawn
being revealed in the Father
and the Father entirely in the Word.

44. O my Jesus, allow me to wash your holy feet; they are
no longer clean when they have journied in my soul.
Permit me to wash away the mud that has bespattered

your steps. But where will I find spring water to wash your feet? I have only my eyes to bathe your feet in my tears; grant that I may also purify myself . . .

Protect your work, O Lord; guard within me the gift you have given . . . Dedicated to the world to begin with, I believed myself unworthy of the episcopate; but because of your grace, I am what I am; but I am the last and the least among the bishops.

As you have set me to work for your Church, bless always the fruit of my labours. You called me to the priesthood, although I was like a lost child; now that I am your priest do not permit that I be lost.

In the first place, give me the grace to be compassionate with sinners from the depths of my heart . . .

The fall of a sinner be a torment to me; may I not be arrogant with him, but weep together with him. Grant that, weeping over my neighbour, I may also weep over myself.

CLAUDIUS CLAUDIANUS

Claudius Claudianus, born in Alexandria in Egypt, lived in Rome from 395, frequenting the imperial court, until 404, in which year we lose all trace of him. His native language was Greek; he learnt his Latin from the study of the classics. He is considered the last notable Latin poet, of a facile and copious vein, but lacking in poetic heart. He celebrated the greatness of Rome, exalting the most illustrious persons of his time; a statue was erected to him in the Trajan Forum. He was a pagan in culture but had felt the fascination of Christianity, and it was probably on this account that the apocryphal songs *Miracles of Christ* and *Praises of Christ* were attributed to him. We give the latter, which reveals a somewhat contorted view in its description of the mystery of redemption and is lacking in true spiritual inspiration.

45. O Christ, true child of God, you are from eternity,
before time began; now begotten; creator of light
before we saw the splendour of your light;
begetter of your Mother;
sent from heaven by the coeternal Father,
you are the one whom the begetting word
sent to dwell within the womb of a Virgin,
within the humble abode of narrow limbs;
you are the one whom no place can contain;
with your first glance you saw
all that you had created at the beginning of the world.

Christ, creator and creature of his own,
accepted life amid the adverse alternation of time
and the weight of its contrasting events.
He bore our human nature to make known God the
    Father,
so that neither the wanton fault, nor the long held
distorted interpretation of the world

could constrain the human mind
to ignorance of its creator through the ages.
The Mother recognised you, conscious of your
    extraordinary birth,
and the flocks acknowledged you with amazed
    apprehension.
The Magi, watching the stars with unquiet eye,
discovered you in the heavens before they found you
by following the splendour of the star.

You set hearts free from sin;
you bring back souls raised in lifeless bodies
commanding them to regain life.
Through the command you received you went down,
    immortal,
to the pathways of the dead, to the souls of the dead.

For you, and you alone, to be born and to die
are not the beginning and the end;
when the darkness had fled you returned to the Father
    in heaven;
and by eternal design, purifying the world,
you made it immune from contagion.

You, the only One, who shares all with the Father;
you, pure Spirit, always one and simple under triple
    name!
In the whole of humanity could there be another?
Who could believe in your death,
when you have power to give back life?

ASTERIUS OF AMASEA

Asterius (?–c. 410), rhetor and lawyer, became bishop of Amasea in Pontus (north of Asia Minor on the Dead Sea). Almost nothing is known of his life; he left some homilies in Greek of a very finished style, having chosen Demosthenes for his model; they draw inspiration from scriptural and liturgical themes, or praise the martyrs and saints, their only aim being the instruction of the faithful. We give below a paschal hymn composed by him.

46. O night clearer than the day!
O night more luminous than the sun!
O night whiter than the snow!
giving more light than our torches,
sweeter than Paradise!
O night that knows no darkness;
driving away our sleep,
you make us keep watch with the angels.
O night, the terror of the demons,
paschal night, awaited for a year!
The Church's wedding night
which gives life to the newly baptised
and renders harmless the torpidity of the demon.
Night in which the Heir
brings the heirs into eternity.

SYNESIUS OF CYRENE

An artistocratic Libyan (?–c. 414) who is one of the strangest figures of Christian antiquity. Refined by the Greek culture he attained in the school of Alexandria, he was elected by popular enthusiasm bishop of Tolemaides even if, like Ambrose, he was not yet baptised. He undertook his pastoral office with zeal, but did not succeed in shaking off completely his former Greco-pagan culture. Besides tracts, sermons and letters, he has left some hymns in the Doric dialect which reveal, within a strange mixture of neo-Platonic ideas and Christian thought, a powerful genius and a vast knowledge. We give two excerpts from his hymns that exactly echo Platonic thought.

47. . . . Christ come among men
as source of light,
your ineffable birth
is before the beginning of time.
You are the radiant light shining with the Father.
You irradiate lustreless matter
and illumine the souls of the faithful.

You have created the world
and fixed the orbit of the stars;
you sustain the axis of the earth,
you save all mankind.
You guide the sun in its course
to light up all our days
and the crescent moon
which dispels the darkness of night.
You make the seed to sprout
preparing food for the flocks.
From your inexhaustible fount
you pour out the splendour of life
making fruitful the whole universe . . .

F

48. I sing to you, blessed and glorious,
Son of the Virgin Mary;
you drove out from the Father's great garden
the serpent of earth
source of all treachery
who offered the accursed fruit,
cause of an unhappy destiny,
as food to the first of men.

Crowned now, and glorious,
Father, Son of the Virgin Mary,
I hymn you.

You descended to earth
to sojourn among mortal men,
bearing a corruptible body.
You descended into tartarus
where death bears rule
over innumerable generations of souls.
There, before you
astonished, the old god
of the underworld
and his cerberus,
devourer of men, . . .
retired from the threshold.
And you set free from their sufferings
the pious choirs of souls . . .
Before you who descended, O Lord,
the infinite race of demons
that people the air, trembled;
astonished was the immortal choir of incorruptible
    stars,
and the glowing firmament,
wise father of harmony,
on his seven stringed lute
added music to the song of victory.

ORIENTIUS

We know neither the date of the birth nor of the death of this ecclesiastical writer. It is certain that he lived in the first part of the 5th century in Gaul (Aquitaine). A poet, imitator of the Latin classics, especially Virgil and Horace, and also Prudentius; two songs of his have come down to us together with some poems rather doubtfully attributed to him.

49. You, Lord, are the holy one and the highest, and you
  bless us.
You are God-Emmanuel, and have dwelt with us.
You are Lord of the universe, and rule over all things.

Israel worships you, and you are worshipped by the
  angels,
the patriarchs, the holy martyrs . . .

Turn your eyes upon us,
O crucified Christ, our consoler,
Nazarene, the God in whom we believe,
God of Galilee, and of our holy father Abraham,
God of Isaac and of Jacob, our faith and our hope.
Keep and defend, O Christ, those you have redeemed.

I, too, beg you; deign to give ear to me,
  almighty:
have pity on me and on mine,
grant that sorrow and fear and anxiety may cease,
join me to your saints and grant that I may fear you
and please you as long as I live,
that I may not be found guilty
in the day when you judge me.
May all my actions honour you
while my mouth gives you praise.

It is known that this Syrian writer (4th century–436), born near Antioch in Syria of pagan parents, was baptised in the Jordan. He became a monk and was elected bishop of Edessa about the year 415. He died in August 436. His few remaining writings consist of a letter of instruction for monks and some hymns that have come down to us in translation.

50. O Christ, bestower of grace and of mercy,
who purifies the sinner from his guilt:
have pity on me.
If it is not easy for the just
to receive the benefit of salvation,
what is there I can do?

I have not borne the burden of the day
nor been burnt by the midday sun:
I am in fact an eleventh hour worker.
Save me, have pity on me.
My sins, throwing me down from the height I had
gained,
have crushed me to the ground,
flung me into the abyss.
Who can lift me up once again
if not you, the creator and infinite wisdom,
who have formed me from my childhood
in your own image and likeness?
By my fault I have become
at one with the demon, the slave of my sin:
set me free, Lord, have pity on me.

Sprinkle me with the dew of your grace;
in your magnanimity, cancel my fault,
Lord, who presides over all things.
Glory be to you.

QUODVULTDEUS

Quodvultdeus, bishop of Carthage (?–c. 453), was a friend and disciple of Augustine. Expelled from Carthage during the invasion of Genseric, king of the Vandals and of Alanus (439), he retired to Campania where he died about the year 453. Among other things some sermons are attributed to him, two of which have been published by the scholarly Cardinal Angelo Mai. The following hymn is taken from the first of the two sermons.

51. Lord, Lord Jesus, you are eternal life
  in the true fatherland, outside time,
  which you have prepared.

  You are the lamp in our Father's house,
  which burns with a suffused light,
  you are the sun of justice,
  the day that knows no ending,
  the shining morning star.

  You alone are temple, priest and victim.
  You alone are the sovereign ruler,
  the lord and the master,
  the creator of brotherhood among men,
  the fount from which springs our peace,
  you are infinite in indulgence.

  All those who belong to you
  will reach the place where you are
  and where you ever will be;
  in the glorious meadows, the leader of the eternal
   dance.

ARMENIAN LITURGY

Evangelised at the dawn of the 4th century by Gregory the Illuminator, Armenia is notable in Christian history as the first nation to receive the Christian religion as a State religion (probably in 314). In its initial phase the Armenian liturgy stemmed from that of Caesarea, as did all other liturgies' evolutions, even that of the Byzantine liturgy. Today the Armenian rite is one of the five principal rites of the Eastern Church. The liturgy now in use dates back to the end of the 5th century, with later additions belonging to the 11th–16th centuries.

We publish an Evening hymn composed before the 10th century which still forms part of the prayer of Vespers.

52. Give to us, O Lord, the peace of the evening
and save us from the snares of the enemy
in the strength of your holy and victorious cross.
> Lord of my salvation,
> I implore you day and night,
> may my prayers come unto you,
> bend your ear to my pleading.
May there come to us, O Lord,
a guardian sent by you
to protect us always.
> Implant in us, O Lord,
> the power of your holy cross
> which will protect us always.
Make us worthy, O Lord,
to spend this evening
in peace and without temptation.
> Deign, O Lord,
> during this night,
> to keep us in peace and without temptation.
The Lord God is with us;
know this, you nations, and be bewildered;

for God is with us.
In him will we hope
and he will be our salvation;
because God is with us . . .
     And the people that dwelt in darkness
     see the great light;
     for God is with us.
And you who live in darkness
and in the shadow of death,
light will shine upon you;
because God is with us.
     And we have been given a Son;
     for God is with us.
And the dominion
will be on his shoulders;
because God is with us.
     And his name will be
     "Messenger of the great mystery";
     for God is with us.
And "Wonderful Counsellor";
because God is with us.
     And "God the strong prince";
     because God is with us.
And the "Prince of peace",
"Father of the world to come";
the "Lord God with us".

AUSONIUS

Ausonius Decimus Magnus (Bordeaux c. 310–395), poet and man of letters, taught grammar and rhetoric in the city, having among his pupils Paulinus of Nola to whom he remained bound by a strong friendship. He was tutor to the Emperor Valerian's son, Gratian, who when he became emperor nominated Ausonius prefect of Gaul and consul. After Gratian's death in 383, he retired into private life in his own city where he devoted himself exclusively to literary studies. He wrote, almost always in verse, epigrams, letters and commemorative discourses. A facile versifier rather than a poet, although a Christian he was at heart a pagan, and was typical in his praise of the world and of culture in which he saw the reason for living. Ausonius is an intellectual, like others of his time, half way betwen Christianity and paganism, in an intermediate position, a zone of shadow which the recent evangelisation had not yet been able to bring wholly into the light. The following prayer is to Christ the Mediator.

53. O God, almighty, always before me,
by the veneration owing to you,
unknown by the wicked but not by the good;
you, without beginning or end;
you are the eternal, before all time that ever was or
    will be;
your nature and your greatness
no human mind can comprehend
or word describe.
Begotten before the morning star
lit up the sky with its golden splendour,
without him nothing was made,
and through him all things were created.
His throne is the heavens
and beneath are the earth

the sea and the deep darkness
of impenetrable night;
ever immovable he governs the universe
and moves all that is without life.
God, begotten of the unbegotten Father,
took upon himself our sins
and suffering for others a terrible death
pointed out the way of return
to life without end.

O Son of the Father all-highest,
Saviour of the world,
to whom is granted
divine power without any reserve
in the fullness of the gift received,
open the way for my prayer,
presenting it to be received
by your Father.
Give me, O Father, the Spirit that I may not turn
    to sin . . .
Free me from the bonds of this frail body,
open to me the ways that lead to the high sphere
of the shining heavens . . .
Give me, O Father, the longed for breath
of eternal light . . .
Grant me pardon
and purify my troubled heart . . .
These vows, made trembling under the weight of sin,
present them, O Son, to the eternal and merciful
    Father;
you, O Saviour, God and Lord,
Spirit, Glory, Word, Son to be believed
begotten of the Truth;
light from light, one with the eternal Father
reigning for all ages.

AUGUSTINE

Augustine Aurelius, born at Tagaste (modern Souk Ahras, in Algeria) in 354, was converted at the age of 33 after a long cultural and spiritual combat testified to in the *Confessions*, and was baptised by Ambrose in Milan. Ordained priest and then bishop of Hippo (now Bona), he had and remained in possession of all the cultural values offered by the civilisation of his time, and was well able to be judge of them. Philosopher, theologian and student of the most profound themes of the faith, defender of orthodoxy against various heretical trends (those of the bishop Donatus and the monk Pelagius and others), as a pastor he was particularly conscious of the ministry of the word, and has left more than 800 sermons. He died in 430. His literary activity was the most copious of the whole of Roman antiquity and occupies fifteen volumes of Migne's *Patrologia Latina*. He is the third of the four great doctors of the Western Church.

54. O sacrament of mercy!
O symbol of unity!
O bond of love!
He who desires life, finds here where to live,
has something to live for.
let him draw near and believe;
let him become part of this body
and he will have life.
Let him not disdain communion with the other
    faithful,
not be a gangrenous member needing amputation,
not be a deformed member of which to be ashamed:
let him be complete, dignified, sound,
profoundly united with the whole body;
let him live with God, for God,
let him now work on earth
and then reign with him in heaven.

MACARIUS THE GREAT

Macarius (d. 390), called the "great" or "the old", lived for sixty years in the desert and was held in exceptional esteem by the monks of Lower Egypt for his wisdom. Many writings are placed under the name of Macarius (ascetic homilies, letters and spiritual sayings). His fifty homilies give him a place among the first mystical writers of Christian antiquity. But the greater part of the literary productions attributed to him would seem to be the work of monks who, out of modesty, hid themselves under his illustrious name.

The evening prayer given here is still used in the Office of None in the Jacobite Church.

55. O God, who came in the fullness of time to save us; you who at the setting of the sun reopened the gates of Heaven to Adam driven forth from Paradise; by the merits of your death on the cross, have pity on me, now that, at the end of my life, nightfall is suddenly upon me. Time is too short to wash away all my guilt. I cannot ask for many more years of life, in which to have time to expiate my innumerable sins.

Spare me, Lord, in the moment of your terrible judgment; have pity on me, O God, on that day, as befits your mercy. Look upon me with a gentle and benevolent eye in the hour of my judgment.

Heal me now, on earth, and I will have the longed for salvation. Raise me up, in your mercy, and lead me to repentance, so that, up above I may see you unashamedly. Do not leave me in the power of my enemies, O Lord, nor let me fall a prey to those who lie in wait for my soul; grant that I may not be deprived either of your grace or of the gift of the Spirit.

O Lord, I will wash the stains from my garments so that I may not be cast out into the outer darkness with those who were considered unworthy to share in the banquet. May my lamp be filled with the oil of good deeds that I may not be counted with the foolish virgins. Spare me, O Lord, from those terrible words spoken to those on your left hand: "I never knew you".

By the blood that you shed for us on the cross, set me free, give me life, according to your mercy, that I may live always in such a way as to testify to your words, to give you glory and to attain to the joy of your kingdom, for ever.
Amen.

SEDULIUS

Celius Sedulius (?–c. 450), was probably born in Italy but passed part of his life in Greece. He was a priest and possibly a bishop. He is the most read and most imitated, along with Prudentius, of all the Latin-Christian poets of the 5th century. He has left five books entitled *Paschal Song* which take up and expand a design for the re-elaboration in hexameters of the most important events of the Old Testament and of the Life of Christ, following the classical schemes (Virgil and Horace). His verse, superabounding in symbolism and rhetorical ornament, restrains poetic inspiration and this results in a harsh translation. The commentary on the "Our Father", which follows, is taken from the *Paschal Song*.

56. He who is desirous of granting our supplications has
taught us how to pray; our kindly-disposed preceptor
exhorts us to express briefly our requests,
that they may swiftly be heard, as we say:

Our Father: ours by virtue of baptism, but his from
all eternity,
even though he grants to man the privilege that is his
very own,
allowing all to have that (divine paternity) which is his
alone.
We call upon the Lord of heaven as our Father
but we cannot be brothers in him
while we cultivate hate for our brothers of human
birth.
Therefore, set ablaze by interior fire,
let us cancel out the heredity that is based on original
error
and show ourselves to be new men, that the happenings
of life
may not cause our separation from our great God

of whom, with Christ to guide us,
we are made adopted sons by divine grace.

Hallowed be your name: and where can the Lord who
    sanctifies be hallowed,
he who made all things, save in a heart that is loving
    and upright?
That we may merit to glorify him with our devotion
he himself has made known to us
how to be honoured, he who is benefactor to all.

Your kingdom come: now; at once, may that kingdom
come ever living, without end and by its eternity not
subject to the passage of time, for it is outside time,
that unending day, without any night,
where Christ reigns;
his noble head haloed with an eternal crown,
the warrior, bearing the arms of victory,
will receive his merited reward.

Your will be done: this, with continuous prayer,
this, day and night, we beg:
that your will be done in heaven and on earth,
for your will is that injustice will be found nowhere,
that nowhere will the temptation of the enemy
    triumph;
thus cast out from heaven and earth,
the sinister serpent will lay no claim to our bodies for
    himself to drag on his length in vile abjection.
May the Almighty, who reconciles all things and
    overflows with goodness, keep safe both souls and
    bodies, for we belong partly to heaven and partly
    to earth.

Give us our daily bread: our faith seeks for nourish-
    ment from daily bread,
that our minds may never be famished for doctrine,
never be without Christ, who with his body and his
    words fills us, being both doctrine and food;
for the words of the Lord in our mouths
are sweeter than honey from the honeycomb.

Forgive us our sins: while we pray that our sins may
    be forgiven
we too should forgive, remembering the demand our
    words lay upon us;
for, if we, once set free (from our sins), refuse
    forgiveness to others,
we will incur the greater condemnation:
if the just Lord, having forgiven us a debt of a
    thousand talents,
comes to hear that we have ill treated a fellow servant
    for ten denarii,
he will quickly hand us over to the executioner
and, chained in a gloomy prison, will not set us free
until we have paid the last farthing.

Lead us not into temptation: not that the Lord, the
    way of light and path of peace,
would lead us into the snares of the tempter, but that
    if it were not for him
we would fall into the snares of evil.
In fact he who, falling into the seductive snares of the
    world,
loves the incense and joys of enticing destruction,
is abandoned by God, the lover of virtue, and goes
    where temptation impels him.
Let us turn our feet back from these paths
and direct our hearts to that difficult journey
on the narrow road that leads to the kingdom of
    heaven.

PAULINUS OF NOLA

Meropius Pontius Paulinus (352–431) was born of a patrician Roman family in Bordeaux (France). He was the favourite pupil of Ausonius (see hymn 53) and was successful in a political career, becoming Consul and Governor of Campania. Receiving baptism at Bordeaux in 396, he gave almost all his patrimony to the poor, and, with his wife's agreement, lived an austere, almost monastic life, first in Spain, where he was ordained priest, and then in Nola (Italy) near the tomb of St Felix (a saint of Syrian origin, bishop of this city for whom Paulinus built a basilica with what remained of his patrimony). He was consecrated bishop of Nola, governing it zealously until his death. Besides his correspondence with the most illustrious persons of his day, Paulinus left important poetic works, including the *Carmina natalicia* in honour of St Felix, and religious and occasional poetry.

57. O Cross, ineffable love of God and glory of heaven!
Cross, eternal salvation; Cross, terror of the reprobate.
O Cross, support of the just, light of Christians,
for you, God became a slave in the flesh, here on earth;
by your means, man in God is crowned king in heaven;
from you streams the true light, victorious over
    accursed night.
You gave believers power to make
the pantheon of the nations quake;
you are the soul of peace
that unites men in Christ the mediator;
you are the ladder for man to climb to heaven.
Be always for us, your faithful, both pillar and anchor;
watch over our homes, set the course of our ship.
In the Cross may our faith remain strong,
and there be our crown prepared.

PRUDENTIUS

Marcus Aurelius Clement Prudentius (c. 348–c. 405) was a native of Calahorra in Spain, where he occupied important political and military posts. Towards the end of his life he retired into solitude to give himself up entirely to God and to poetry, in order to — as he wrote — expiate his faults. His poetic works, of true religious lyrical and didactic inspiration, put him in the first rank among Western Christian hymn writers.

58. A festive chirrupping announces the day,
singing in the light of dawn.
Christ spurs on the soul,
inviting us to a rebirth, this day.

Arise from your beds, he urges,
where a feeble languor makes you inert.
Be watchful, chaste, good, and sober;
for I am close to you.

Let us invoke Jesus, aloud,
sorrowing, praying, repentant;
an ardent invocation
keeps a pure heart on the alert.

O Christ, drive away sleep,
break the chains of night,
make good the ancient fault,
bring to us new light.

Glory be to God the Father,
and to his only Son,
together with the Spirit, the consoler,
now and for ever.

G

AMBROSIAN LITURGY

The Sacramentaries are books which contain the prayer formulae of the first Christian assemblies and they offer a collection of Prefaces (the prayer which precedes the central portion of the eucharistic celebration). As with other prayers, initially the celebrant was allowed to compose the preface but later, with the birth of formulae composed for the purpose, it became practically fixed. The prefaces attributed in the various codices to the Ambrosian liturgy are about 300; the oldest (about 76 of them) are pre-6th century and plainly demonstrate their Milanese origin. They exhibit a richness in respect of the Roman and other Western liturgies. These prefaces, brief compositions which draw inspiration from the events of the Gospel or hagiography, unfold the praise of God for his goodness, because "it is right and dutiful and the source of salvation".

We give here the prefaces for the Epiphany and for Easter.

59. [Father]
On the banks of the Jordan your voice resounded
in the roll of thunder coming from heaven
making manifest the Saviour,
showing yourself as Father of eternal light.
You have rent the heavens,
blessed the air,
purified the water,
made manifest your only Son
through the Holy Spirit
appearing in the form of a dove.
Today the fountains, having received your blessing,
cast off the ancient curse;
and so, the faithful, purified from their sins,
are presented to God, for eternal life,
as sons by adoption.
In fact those who through birth in the flesh
were destined for the life of time,

those whom death had seized through the complicity
    of sin
are welcomed into eternal life
and brought back to the glory of heaven.

60. It is necessary, and for our well-being, to give you
    thanks
God, holy and almighty,
to celebrate your praise with devotion, Father of glory,
creator and author of the universe,
through your Son, Jesus Christ.
He, being God, full of majesty, humbled himself
to the point of accepting the punishment of the cross
for the salvation of men.
In the depth of ages
Abraham prefigured this in his son;
the people of Moses with the paschal lamb they
    immolated.
He it is of whom
announcement was made by the voice of the prophets:
he would take upon himself the sins of all men,
cancel out the whole of our misdeeds.
This is the great Pasch
which the blood of Christ has covered with glory,
making the Christian people exult with joyous
    devotion!
O mystery of grace!
Inexpressible mystery of divine munificence!
O festival most venerated among all festivals,
in which he abandoned himself to men
even unto death, to save mere slaves!
O blessed death, which has broken the chains of death!
Now the prince of hell is vanquished,
and we, saved from the abyss of guilt,
exult in joy and take with Christ once more
the road to heaven.

ENNODIUS

Magnus Felix Ennodius (c. 474–521), born in Gaul, educated in the pagan schools of **Pavia** and **Milan**, was converted to Christianity and later became bishop of Pavia. He was the author, among other things, of an autobiography on the lines of the *Confessions* of Augustine and of two books of *Songs*, comprising occasional poems, descriptions of journeys, hymns and epigrams. The whole of his production displays an artificial attempt to reconcile pagan art with Christian spirituality. This is apparent in the hymn we give, in which excessive use of rhetorical devices takes from its sincerity and efficacy.

61. The links of the chain are all broken;
　　　the serpent is robbed of his venom;
　　　the meek tramples on pride;
　　　the lion is torn by the lamb.

　　　This is a sign of great power, O Christ,
　　　that you take upon yourself the guilt,
　　　and, hidden in the garments of a slave,
　　　lead us on to triumph,
　　　as if, from your sparkling throne,
　　　with your thunder you were striking terror in kings.
　　　God is revealed in all,
　　　if we do not hide away from him,
　　　for, to raise up those lying on their backs
　　　he abased himself to become
　　　even that which we are;
　　　he himself came to save
　　　that which was already his.
　　　He brought back the wandering sheep
　　　to the sheepfold of the shepherd.

　　　Raise the gates, O you angels:
　　　the terrible judge enters in
　　　higher than the monuments of victory of the foe.

THE RAVENNA SCROLL

Discovered by the scholars A. Ceriani and Count G. Porro in the Ferrara Archives of Falco Pio, belonging to the Prince Antonio Pio of Savoy, and published in 1883, the scroll is of worn parchment (360 cms long and 19 cms wide) damaged at both ends. It is written on both sides in a careful, regular script, and some of the initials and more important words are in red: on the recto side there are some liturgical prayers; on the reverse, some letters exchanged between the bishop of Ravenna and various people of his time, among whom was Sergius, pope between 904 and 911. This gives ground to suppose its provenance is the Church of Ravenna. The 42 prayers, authentic jewels of the religious patrimony, were probably used at Mass and at the principal Hours of the canonical office during Advent. Exegesis of the formulae reveals a notable linguistic and thematic affinity with some prayers of the primitive Roman liturgy (4th–5th century), from the proper of the Nativity of the Lord. The prayers contained in the scroll belong to different periods and authors but according to the most informed opinion they are recognisable as belonging to the ambit of the Churches in the area of Padua and chronologically to the time between the end of the first and the beginning of the fifth centuries. The scroll is now preserved in the Ambrosian Library of Milan.

62. O almighty God, hear the prayer of your people,
that justice radiating from heaven
may cloak the whole earth with justice.
We pray to you, that our souls,
anxiously awaiting,
may, at the coming of your Son, the redeemer of the
world,
be filled to overflowing with every blessing.

63. O God, you are the way of truth
and ineffable mystery of unity in trinity:
implant in us, in your kindness, your operative grace,

that, with meritorious works,
    we may be able to go to the encounter with our
    Saviour who comes,
and so share in the reward of beatitude.

64. Eternal Lord, Son of God,
who, by the inexplicable mystery of your incarnation,
made the mountains exult,
and the hills leap with joy,
grant us the gift not to fear you
in your second coming,
but freed from the chains of sin,
may recognise the Redeemer of the human race,
whom we proclaim with sincere faith
God and Lord of the angels.

65. O God, who at the beginning of the world,
creating light, dispelled the impenetrable clouds
of darkness, we pray you:
May the creator of light come quickly,
the promise of that true marriage bed
prepared from all eternity,
that your people,
freed from the ancient snare,
may go to the encounter with your Son
worthily prepared.

66. O God, hidden beneath a human form,
who, in birth, left intact
the virginal prerogative of your mother,
we pray you:
Come quickly, Redeemer of the human race
and Saviour of the world;
then, adoring the double nature of your glory
with faith intact we will cry
hosanna to you, one and only majesty,
who lives and reigns, God, for ever and ever.

ROMANOS THE MELODIOUS

Romanos was born about 490 in Emesa in Syria (now Homs)
and received from his family an excellent Christian education.
To complete his studies he moved to Berito (modern Beirut),
at that time the most important intellectual centre in Syria. He
was ordained deacon for life. He then went to Constantinople
where he settled close to a Marian shrine in the city, giving
his services as deacon and preacher, and remaining there until
his death which occurred sometime between 555 and 562.

Romanos is considered to be the greatest poet of the Byzantine
Church, where he is also venerated as a saint. Legendary
hagiography says that he received his poetic gift directly from
Our Lady. It is certain that Romanos composed an enormous
number of hymns, few of which have come down to us, which
testify to his talent, his spiritual and artistic sensibility, and the
form of preaching, unique of its kind, which he adopted; that
is, he preached entirely in verse, with a frequent refrain which
the people were invited to repeat to express their own assent.

Romanos, preacher and poet, was more concerned with being a
catechist rather than a theologian; his intention was to lead his
people to live a Christian life; his, then, is a popular type of
preaching which, however, did not fail to reach the heights of
mysticism.

67. My Saviour, you have taken my condition on yourself
    that I may approach to yours.
    You have accepted your passion,
    that I may despise evil desires.
    Your death has brought me to birth in new life.
    You were laid in the grave
    and for me you keep Paradise for my home.
    Descending into hell, you have raised me up;
    throwing down the gates of hell
    you have opened for me the gates of heaven.
    You have endured through the guilt of fallen man,
    have suffered for the salvation of Adam.

68. As the man born blind, deprived of the eyes of the
soul
I come to you, O Christ,
crying out in my compunction:
"You are the shining light
to those who are in darkness".

O Saviour, pour out upon me
the torrent of ineffable wisdom
and of sublime knowledge;
O light of those who dwell in night,
guide the one who has gone astray, so that I,
    wretched that I am,
may be empowered to recount your marvels,
as we have learned from the divine book,
the Gospel of peace,
through the miracle of the blind man;
that is, like the one who was infirm from his birth,
received eyes of flesh,
and at the same time eyes for the soul,
may I cry out in faith:
"You are the shining light
to those who are in darkness".

69. You came, O Lord, to the tomb of Lazarus,
and raised him to life from the dead after three days,
putting shackles on hell, O Almighty.
Seized with compassion for the tears of Mary and
    Martha,
you spoke to them thus:
"He will show himself, he will rise from the tomb
saying: 'You are the life and the resurrection'."
We weep, thinking of death
and those who are dead;
but we should not;
for we know from where they have gone,
and where they are now
and in whose hands they rest:
they have departed from this ephemeral life,

freed from their pains;
they are at rest waiting to be illumined by God.
He who holds them in his hand
is the Friend of men,
who has taken away their ephemeral garments
to reclothe them in a body of eternity.
Why then do we mourn without reason?
Why do we not believe Christ who has said:
"He who believes in me will never die"?
For, even if he should see corruption,
after the corruption, without change, man will be
      remade
and will rise up, saying:
"You are the life and the resurrection".

70. O God of mercy,
you who feed us with your flesh,
free us from hunger and from every misery,
O Christ, you who are our God;
and deign, at the prayer of the Mother of God,
to give us your everlasting gifts,
for you are, O Saviour,
the heavenly bread of immortality.

All the angels of heaven
are amazed at what they see on earth,
for men, made of the earth,
and living here below,
are lifted up in the spirit and raised on high
participating with the crucified Christ.
Because all together are eating of this body,
given to adoration of the bread of life,
and hoping for eternal salvation.
If to the senses it is a visible bread,
it sanctifies spiritually,
because it is the heavenly bread of immortality.

The bread which we eat is the flesh of the Emmanuel:
the Master himself first taught us this:

in the hour in which of his own will
he went forth to his passion,
Christ broke the bread of salvation
and said to his apostles, as it is written:
"Come now, and eat it,
and, as you eat, you will receive eternal life;
for this food is truly my flesh
because I — you do see me —
am the heavenly bread of immortality".

POPE PELAGIUS I

Pope Pelagius I was born in Rome at an unknown date and died in 561. In 536 he was already a deacon, close to Pope Agapitus, in the unhappy years when the Church was under the heavy hand of the Emperor Justinian. When Rome was occupied by Totila, king of the Goths, Pelagius was present and confronted him, demanding clemency for the people. He was elected pope upon designation by the emperor, and this brought on him much adversity. However, during his brief pontificate he tried hard to bring the Roman clergy together again, to repair churches and to stimulate works of charity. He is buried in St Peter's.

71. Have pity, O Christ,
  on those who believe in you.
  You are the God of glory
  for all ages.
    Hasten to the aid of those who suffer,
    make speed to comfort those in trouble.
  Father of believers, life of the living,
  God who is over all, for there is no-one above you.
    Creator of all things, universal judge,
    Lord over princes, God of the world.
  Sublime majesty of the heavenly Jerusalem,
  king, glory, and triumph of the kingdom.
    God of eternal light, inexpressible,
    highest, most loveable, beyond compare.
  Great and clement God, wise and omniscient,
  mover of all things, ancient and new.

VENANTIUS FORTUNATUS

Venantius Fortunatus, was born near Treviso in 540 and died at Poitiers in France a little after 600; he was bishop of that city. He was a court poet; then, being ordained priest, he became spiritual director of a monastic community of women. His culture brought him to know other learned men of his time. A great number of his poems, epitaphs, hymns and elegies, almost all of Christian inspiration, have come to us. Among his hymns the most well-known are the *Vexilla Regis prodeunt*, translated below, and the *Pange lingua*, still in use in the liturgy.

72. The regal banners now advance,
   now shines the mystery of the cross
   on which the Creator of mankind
   made man, was raised on high to die.

> With arms fast bound and nailed hands
> the cross-piece fixed, we now behold
> the sign of our redemption there
> where Clemency the victim makes.

His side, sore wounded by the point,
transpiercing, of the cruel lance,
to cleanse the world from sinful stain
pours blood and water from the wound.

> Now is the prophecy fulfilled
> of David speaking with such truth
> when to the nations he foretold
> that God would reign upon a tree.

O shining and majestic tree
adorned with regal mantle now,
most noble trunk, chosen to bear
limbs of such great sanctity.

O blessed tree, that with your arms
support the Saviour of the world
a balance for that flesh divine
that snatched away the prey of hell.

From your bark a perfume breathes
in sweetness surpassing nectar far,
proudly you bear the fertile fruit
while shouts acclaim his triumph now.

From the glory of the Passion
praise to the altar and Victim blest
in passion, undergoing death,
with death, restoring life again.

Hail cross, our one and only hope,
in this our time of mourning, grant
that all the faithful grow in grace
and sinners have their guilt forgiv'n.

O Trinity, the source of life,
all spirits sing their praise to you.
To those time-bound give comfort still,
who by the cross have been redeemed.

73. Hail, happy day, festival for all the peoples,
the day when God, hell vanquished, conquered heaven!
Behold the gratitude of new-born creation,
with all his gifts, to the returning Lord.
To Christ, indeed, returned from the desolate realm
of the dead,
all things render their homage due;
the wood with all its leafy branches,
the meadow with its flowers.
You are the Lord, who, seeing the human race plunged
into the abyss,
to save man became yourself a man.
Thus were the weighty chains of the law of
death all broken;
in its confusion the universe was thus restored
by the radiance of your face.

I pray you, O Majesty most kind, fulfill the
  promise:
day has broken, arise, O my Christ, from the
  tomb where you lay.
Drive back the endless darkness of the infernal
  dungeons
and raise up on high all that has fallen into the
  abyss.
Turn again your face to us, that future ages may be
  filled with your light,
and bring back the day to those who without you
  would have lost it for ever.

The Hibernian-Celtic hymnody forms part of the manifestations of barbaric cultures which developed in the area of Latin literature in Ireland and England at the height of the Middle Ages. In the Church of these regions many penitential books were written (minutely regulating the penances to be applied to different sins) and it is from this atmosphere, with its sense of sin and widespread penitential spirit, that we cull the following prayer.

74. Pardon, Lord; pardon your people
whom you have redeemed with your blood, O Christ;
may your anger not weigh upon us.
> We pray you for your infinite clemency;
> turn away your wrath from this city
> and from your holy house.

We have sinned against you
and you have been angry with us
and no one can flee from your punishments.
> We have sinned against you, O Lord,
> we have sinned.
> Be merciful to us, set us free from ills
> which every day fall upon us.

Pardon, O Lord, the sins of your people,
according to your infinite generosity.
> You once showed kindness to our fathers:
> be merciful to us and your glory
> will shine out in our lives.

Pardon, O Lord, those who have sinned;
give your grace to those who repent;
have pity on us who pray to you,
O Christ, Saviour of the world.
> Jesus, look upon us
> and have pity. Amen.

COLUMBAN

Columban (c. 543–615) was born in Ireland. He entered the most famous Benedictine monastery of his time, at Bangor (see hymn 87), where he was a disciple of the great abbot Comgall. Towards the year 590, following the tradition of the Irish monks pilgrims "for Christ" on all the roads of Europe — Columban left the island and set out to cross Brittany and Gaul, founding monasteries in the Vosges of which he was abbot. He was surrounded by twelve companions among whom was Gall, later the founder of the monastery that still bears his name in the Swiss canton of St Gall, near Constance. The persecutions of the Frankish clergy, intolerant of Irish innovations introduced into the liturgy and ecclesiastical discipline, indicated to him what would be his mission. Columban turned to Pope Gregory I for justification of his work, but the persecution continued and Columban and his monks were imprisoned and sent back to Ireland.

During the voyage, they succeeded in escaping, and after various journeyings, arrived in Milan where they received protection at the Longobard court of Agilulfo and Theodolinda. Having become counsellor to the queen, Columban devoted himself by word and writing to the anti-Arian struggle. In 614 he founded the monastery of Bobbio in the Appenines, one of the liveliest centres of spirituality and culture of medieval times. Columban left works that witness to his remarkable degree of culture: homilies, monastic rules, epistles and poetry of noble inspiration (the authenticity of some is questioned).

75. Blessed and happy "are those servants, who, at their Lord's return, will be found watching" (Lk 12:37)! Blessed is that watch in which God himself is waited, the creator of the universe who fills all things and transcends them all! Heaven grant that the Lord will shake even me, his wretched servant, from the torpor of my laziness and inflame me with his divine charity so as to set me on fire with his love, even more

than the stars, so that I may burn with desire to love him more and more, and this fire may never be extinguished in me! . . .

Heaven grant that my merits may be great enough for my lamp to burn all night in the temple of the Lord, to give light to those who come into the house of my God.

God my Father, I pray you, in the name of your Son Jesus Christ, give me charity that will never fail, that my torch may be always alight, and never burn out; heat for me and a shining light for others.

Deign, O Christ, our most gentle Saviour, to light our lamps; may they burn constantly in your temple, fed by you, who are the eternal light; may the dark corners of our spirit be lit up and the darkness of this world flee far from us.

Give then, O Jesus, I pray you, a light to my lamp that by its rays the heavenly sanctuary will be visible to me . . .

Grant that I may see and contemplate and desire you alone; you alone may I love, always fervently awaiting you . . .

O beloved Saviour, show yourself to us who knock, that knowing you, we may love you alone, desire only you, think always of you alone, meditating day and night on your words. Awaken in us such a love as may be rightly and fittingly rendered to you.

O God, may your love take possession of our whole being and make it totally yours . . .

MAXIMUS

Maximus, saint and confessor (580–652), was born at Constantinople and dedicated himself to serious study, especially of philosophy. He was called to the imperial court to fill the post of first secretary, but abandoned it at the age of 34 to become a monk. Persecuted by the supporters of heresy, imprisoned, tortured and mutilated in the tongue and arm, he was finally sent into exile in the region of Batum (to the east of the Black Sea) where he died after two years. He left about sixty volumes of exegesis and ascetical writing.

76. My Saviour, grant that the arduous task of my
    salvation may be brought to a happy conclusion.
May neither the lashing rains,
nor the impetus of torrents racing down from the
    mountains,
nor the violent storm be able to shake my house.

With your victorious hand, assist me, Lord!
Be my help, preserve my life,
that I may praise you, the giver and Lord of all that
    is most precious
and the salvation of men.

Without you, Almighty, no work would exist,
no project, no idea, no proposal, no security,
nor any of those things that
would serve to attain the final end.

You have created and given me, both soul and body;
you have raised me up when I had fallen,
and have shown me the way to heaven.

And you will bring me in, without merit of mine,
to your house to live with you in eternity
and to sing a hymn to your glory
along with all the blessed.

MOZARABIC LITURGY

Its name derives from the adjective meaning "to be made arabic", and was given by the Arabs, during their occupation, to Christian Spaniards. The liturgy, however, in spite of this adjective, is Western in essence. It is also called Visigothic or Hispanic. Originally it drew from the Latin literary culture of the Spain of the 7th and 8th centuries, continuing to the end of the 12th. Dense in concepts and expressed in a sumptuous rite, it is now preserved only in the Cathedral of Toledo.

77. We praise you, Lord Jesus Christ,
God-Saviour of men,
stupendously powerful with the Father;
we praise you, we invoke you, we pray to you;
assist us with your pardon, with clemency give us
    your grace.

Awaken in our hearts desires deserving of fulfilment;
suggest to us words that are worthy to be heard;
grant that our actions may be worthy of blessing.

We beg you to renew your birth in human nature,
penetrating us with your invisible godhead
as you did in a unique way in Mary
and do now spiritually in the Church.

May you be conceived by our faith,
that a mind untouched by corruption may bring you
    forth,
that the soul, ever confirmed by the power of the
    Most High,
may offer you a dwelling place.

Be not born in us, but reveal yourself in us.
Be truly for us the Emmanuel, God with us.
Deign to remain with us, to fight for us,
Only so can we conquer.

78. Christ, you are alpha and omega, the beginning and
the end;
you consecrate this sacrifice offered to you
at the beginning of the new year,
and inscribe the names of all those who offer it
in the book of life;
you also grant the dead eternal rest;
may we who celebrate the beginning
of this year with joyful praise
be found worthy to pass the rest of its course
in your service.

Bless, O Lord, the last part of the year,
gift of your kindness, that your fields
may overflow with generous fertility
and we who sojourn in this valley of tears
may rejoice in the abundance of the joys of peace.

O Holy and Omnipotent, to you we pray:
grant true light to your faithful ones,
that it may not happen that, deprived of your light,
they fall into ruin, not knowing
that which is reserved for them this day,
allotted to them as a gift of great kindness.

May we, who have been gathered together,
receive the holy mysteries.
May all stain be washed from body and soul,
and hearts be shining with true light,
and with your aid may we long be secure.

Let us also beg the Lord's clemency
that his divine help may come to us from heaven;
and united with the company of the angels
and with hearts shining in innocence,
we may journey with grace renewed.

79. Come to us, Jesus, as we pray in your temple, and
help us . . .
Behold, we uncover our wounds
before the glory of your name:
provide a remedy for our ills.
Help us, according to the promise made to those who
pray to you,
those whom you have drawn from nothing.
Make ready the ointment and apply it
to the eyes of the heart and of the body,
that we may no longer wobble in the dark like the
blind.
Behold, we pour out our tears at your feet,
do not drive us far away, now that we are humbled.
Good and humble Jesus, who have come down to
earth,
we will not stray from your way.
Hear our prayer,
uproot the sin that makes us blind:
then we will contemplate the glory of your face
and praise you in the peace of endless beatitude.

80. O Christ, you are the light of day;
you drive away the clouds of night;
for us, your faithful, you are light of light
which, by your gift, fills us with blessedness.

God of holiness, we invoke your protection
during this night.
You are our true repose,
grant that we may sleep in peace.

Guard us from nightmares
and the snares of the enemy.
Preserve spotless our bodies
and our conscience without stain.

When sleep closes our eyelids
may our hearts still watch,
may your hand protect the faithful
who declare to you their love.

117

Watch over us, O our protector.
Drive danger far away;
guide the servants
whom you have redeemed.

Lord, you who are the guardian
of our souls, abandon not
those weighed down by the burden of the body.
Remain with us, O Lord.

THE VENERABLE BEDE

Bede, saint and doctor of the Church (673–735), English like Alcuin, is considered, if not the greatest, one of the most learned men of the Middle Ages. At the age of 7 he was offered to a monastery and remained there until his death. The major part of his work consists of biblical exegesis. The better part of his work, considered from the stylistic and literary point of view, consists in historical works, in particular the history of the Anglosaxon Church. Venerated as a saint soon after his death, he was proclaimed doctor of the Church by Pope Leo XIII.

81. Remain, O Christ, in the hearts you have redeemed;
You who are perfect love,
pour into our words
sincere repentance.

We raise our prayer to you,
O Jesus, with faith;
pardon the sin we have committed.

By the holy sign of the cross,
by your tortured body,
defend us constantly as your sons.

ANDREW OF CRETE

Byzantine monk, orator and hymn writer (c. 660–740), he was at first a simple monk in the laura (monastery) of St Sabas near Jerusalem, later he became a cleric. About the year 700 he was elected archbishop of Gortina, a city in the island of Crete. He spent himself in the struggle against the monothelite heresy (which claimed that there was only one will in Christ, without distinguishing between his divine and human wills), and in the defence of the cult of icons. As a hymn writer, he was the first to put the canons of the Mass into poetical dress.

82. O Mother of God, your lap became the holy table
whereon would rest the heavenly bread,
of which whoever eats will never die,
according to the word of him who nourishes all . . .

And you, O Jesus, with five loaves, satisfied the
    thousands starving;
and with the remains could feed yet thousands more,
revealing thus your glory to your faithful disciples.

He who eats of your bread will live for ever,
and he who drinks your blood will dwell in you,
and you will dwell in him
and raise him up on the last dread day.

83. A room on the upper floor
provided with table and napery,
welcomed you, the Creator, and your companions,
and there you celebrated the paschal mystery,
for there, two of your disciples
had prepared for you the Pasch . . .
Happy those who can receive the Lord in faith;
their hearts prepared as upper room,
sentiments of love as food to offer you . . .

Taking food, O Lord, with your disciples
you showed forth mystically your holy death
by which we are redeemed from all corruption,
we who honour your venerable passion . . .
O lover of mankind,
sitting at supper with your disciples;
you revealed to them the great mystery of your
    incarnation,
saying: Eat the bread that gives you life,
drink the blood in faith,
that flows out from the pierced side divine.
The upper room,
where Christ celebrated the Pasch,
was transformed into a heavenly tabernacle;
the banquet without blood;
the cult, that of the spirit;
the table whereon the mysteries had been celebrated,
an altar, acceptable to the mind.
Christ is the Pasch, the Pasch great and holy;
eaten as bread and sacrificed as lamb,
he is the victim offered up for us;
Let us all receive mystically,
with sentiments devout,
his body and his blood.

JOHN DAMASCENE

Born at Damascus, in Syria, about 675 of a family of func-
tionaries in the service of the Byzantine government and also
of the dominating Islamic power. He received an adequate
education and filled important civil posts. About 718 he
embraced the monastic life, and later, having received the
priesthood, gave himself up immediately and intensely to
preaching and writing. At his death in 749 he left abundant
writings in the fields of theology, exegesis, ascetism and liturgy.
His many hymns, still part of the patrimony of the Byzantine
Church, place him among the great hymn writers of that
Church's liturgy.
We give excerpts from his eucharistic prayers.

84. Lord Jesus Christ, our God,
   who alone has the power
   to forgive the sins of men,
   who are so good and merciful to men,
   do not take into account
   my many failings, conscious or unconscious,
   and make me worthy to receive,
   without fear of condemnation,
   your divine, glorious, and immaculate mysteries
   which give life.
   May this communion not be for me a cause of
         punishment,
   or increase my sin,
   but be my purification, sanctification,
   the pledge of the future kingdom;
   may it be my defence,
   may it help to bring my enemies to nothing;
   may it cancel out my many sins,
   for you are the God of mercy,
   of indulgence, and of love for men;

122

to you we give glory, with the Father
and the Holy Spirit
through all ages to come.

85. I stand before the door of your church
and cannot shake off my evil thoughts.
But you, O Christ,
who have justified the publican,
had compassion on the Canaanite woman,
opened the gate of paradise to the dying thief,
open to me the treasures of your bounty,
and, as I draw near and touch you,
welcome me as you welcomed the sinner
and the sick woman whom you had cured.
For, the one who had touched
but the hem of your robe received health,
and she who had embraced your feet without stain
obtained pardon for her sins.
And I, wretched as I am, who burn to receive
the whole of your body,
may I not be flung into the flames,
but receive me as you received them,
and enlighten my soul,
pardoning my faults,
through the intercession of the Virgin who bore you,
and of the heavenly powers;
may you be blessed for all ages to come.

86. My heart is pierced, I am consumed with ardour
    for you,
my love for you has transformed me, O Lord;
I am the prisoner of your love.
May I be filled with your flesh,
inebriated with your blood
which gives life, the very life of God;
may I rejoice in your gifts,
immersed in the joy

your divinity gives;
and, when you return in glory,
may I be worthy to meet you
and be carried up beyond the clouds of the air,
united with all your elect, to praise you,
give you glory, and thanks, and witness,
together with the Father, who has no beginning,
and the life-giving Holy Spirit . . .

BANGOR ANTIPHONARY

Ireland, evangelised at the beginning of the 5th century, rapidly developed an intense monastic life. Its monasteries were not only centres of faith and ascetism, but also of a vigorous culture; and its monks were the fervent missionaries of the island before the Roman missionaries sent by Pope Gregory the Great in 597 arrived. There was plenty of scope in the Irish monasteries for the study of the classics, the Bible and the Fathers, as well as for the national culture. Among the texts which witness to the life and religious and cultural fervour of Ireland's monasteries, is, among others, the Bangor Antiphonary, the oldest liturgical book in the island. Bangor was an important abbey, founded in 557 by St Comgall (it was destroyed in the 10th century but rebuilt and reformed, though today there is nothing left of it). Columban was formed at Bangor and his continental mission began there. The Antiphonary, which dates back to the 7th century, is one of the most notable documents of Celtic liturgy. It was discovered in the Monastery of Bobbio and acquired by Cardinal Federico Borromeo for the Ambrosian Library. It was studied and published for the first time by L. A. Muratori in 1713.

We transcribe the canticle for the priest's communion.

87. Come, O faithful,
   eat of the body of Christ
   and receive the most holy blood
   by which you were redeemed.

   Let us praise God,
   we, who have been saved by the body
   and the blood of Christ,
   and gain strength from him.

   By this sacrament
   of the body and blood
   we are all of us set free
   from the mouth of hell.

Christ, the Son of God
and minister of salvation,
saved the world
by the cross and by his blood.

Immolated for us all
the Lord became
both priest and victim . . .

The giver of light
and saviour of all
has granted to his children
a singular grace.

Let all the faithful draw near
and, in hearts that are pure,
receive the eternal pledge
of their salvation . . .

The guardian of the saints
is guide and lord
of eternal life, which
he gives to the faithful.

He gives heavenly bread
to those who desire it
and quenches their thirst
from a living fountain.

Christ the Lord,
alpha and omega,
has come and will return
to judge mankind.

Alcuin, born in England about 735, died at Tours in France in 804. Of a noble Anglosaxon family, he was a disciple of the Archbishop of York. He was ordained deacon and given charge of the "Schola" (the first university of that city), whose prestige and fame he augmented. During a mission to Rome he met the Emperor Charlemagne at Parma, who persuaded him, under vigorous pressure, to stay with him as counsellor. In a short time he became the emperor's preceptor in all the sciences. His culture in fact was multiform, and his vast literary output ranged from philosophy and theology to history and rules of poetry. As an outstanding member of the French liturgical school he resisted the acceptance of Roman liturgical books.
We give a prayer to Christ from the *Liturgical Collection* which bears his name.

88. We beg you, good Jesus, our Lord,
by the intercession of the glorious Virgin Mary
your Mother, and of all the angels and saints,
to increase the faith of your catholic Church,
to grant us peace and forgive our sins.

Grant health to the sick,
a good journey and happy arrival
to those who travel by land or sea,
serenity to those who suffer,
liberty to the oppressed;
to slaves, to the vanquished, to pilgrims,
liberty, clemency and return to their homeland.

Send your holy angel on sentry
over those who place obstacles to fraternal charity;
in your kindness grant true faith to those who believe
not,
and eternal repose to those of our brothers
who have died in the faith.

GALLICAN FORMULARIES

In classical antiquity a form of literary composition was known which consisted in collecting together passages in prose and verse and phrases of well known authors, and was called "patchwork". This literary exercise was also practised by the Christians of the first centuries who made a "patchwork" of prayers, homilies and treatises from the first Fathers, thus composing formulae for prayer in the community assembly. Substantially these prayer formulae were of individual inspiration, due to the celebrant or his assistants or a versed lay person. They varied from Church to Church, and when they became common, were collected in codices called formularies. Today these formularies are precious for the history of liturgy.

89. Lord Jesus, I give you thanks,
   not only with the lips and heart,
   which often comes to little, but with the spirit,
   with which I speak to you, question you,
   love you, and recognise you.
   You are my all, and everything is in you.
   In you we live, and move, and have our being.

   You are our father, our brother, our all;
   and to those who love you, you have promised such
      things
   as no one has ever seen or thought of,
   no one ever enjoyed.

   Make the gift of these things to your humble faithful;
   you who are God, true and good,
   and there is no other besides you.

   You are the true God, the true Son of God,
   to whom be honour and glory and majesty
   in eternity and for all ages to come.

90. Lord Jesus Christ, I adore you,
because you said at the beginning of time:
"Let there be light" and the light shone forth.
May your light, O Lord, be salvation for me.

Lord Jesus Christ, I adore you,
you wept over Lazarus and raised him from the dead;
I beg that I may gain eternal life,
and that you will cause to spring up within me
your fountain of living water,
gushing out for eternal life.

Lord Jesus Christ, I adore you,
transfixed to the cross,
wine and myrrh to quench your thirst:
I beg that your wound may be transformed
into a medicine for my soul.

Lord Jesus Christ, I adore you, laid in the tomb:
May your death be life to me.

91. August creator of the world, Lord Jesus Christ, equal
and co-eternal with the Father and the Holy Spirit in
the splendour of their glory, yet who deigned to take
flesh in the womb of an immaculate Virgin, and
allowed your wondrous hands to be pierced by nails
on the cross in order to throw open the gates of hell
and set free the human race from eternal death, look
upon me with mercy, who am so miserable, disgraced
and crushed by such a weight of sin.

Most clement Father, do not abandon me, but be
indulgent to me who have behaved so wickedly.

Prostrate in adoration before your cross, hear me;
that I may merit this day to come to you, purified and
welcome to your eyes; and so, set free from all evil,
to be always supported by your aid, received from
your loving kindness, O Christ, Saviour of the world.

The Byzantine rite, more than any other Christian rite, reserves a very special place for the cult of the cross. The liturgical books of the Byzantine Church overflow with hymns, generally short, referring to the cross and Christ crucified. The texts were composed by the Eastern Fathers from the 6th to the 9th centuries. To us, far away from the Eastern mentality, and generally given to expressing our faith in a measured and detached way, the warmth of this expression of praise may seem too much for our prayer. We present two hymns to Christ crucified.

92. By the tree of the cross
you have healed the bitterness of the tree,
and have opened Paradise to men.
Glory be to you, Lord!

Now we are no longer prevented
from coming to the tree of life;
we have hope in your cross.
Glory be to you, Lord!

O Immortal One, nailed to the wood,
you have triumphed over the snares of the devil.
Glory be to you, Lord!

You, who for my sake have submitted
to being placed on the cross,
accept my vigilant celebration of praise,
O Christ, God, Friend of men.

Lord of the heavenly armies,
who knows my carelessness of soul,
save me by your cross,
O Christ, God, Friend of men.

Brighter than fire, more luminous than flame,
have you shown the wood of your cross, O Christ.
Burn away the sins of the sick and enlighten the hearts
of those who, with hymns, celebrate

your voluntary crucifixion.
Christ, God, glory to you!

Christ, God,
who for us accepted a sorrowful crucifixion,
accept all who sing hymns to your passion,
and save us.

93. Lord, nailed to the cross,
at your sight the sun lost its brightness,
the veil of the temple was torn,
the earth trembled, the rocks split apart,
not being able to bear the sight of the Creator
unjustly suffering upon the tree
and insulted by the wicked.

You have allowed yourself to be judged,
sole king who will judge the universe on your return;
you have received a crown of thorns, O Saviour,
but by your power
you pluck out the thorns of falsehood,
and in all those who adore your crucifixion
you implant the knowledge of your mercy.

Save me, Christ Saviour,
by the power of your cross,
you who saved Peter from the sea,
and have pity on me, O God.

The tree of your cross, Christ God,
has become the tree of life for those who believe.
By it, defeating the power of death,
you have given us life, who were dead through
    our sins.
Therefore we cry to you:
Lord, strength of the universe, glory to you!

Christ God,
you have wrought salvation in the midst of the earth,
you have stretched out your most pure arms on the
    cross,
reuniting all peoples who cry out:
Glory to you, O Lord!

RABANUS MAURUS

A theologian and ecclesiastical writer (Magonza 784–856), a disciple of Alcuin in the School of Tours, he was ordained priest in the abbatial monastery of Fulda and later himself became Abbot (822). Consecrated bishop of Magonza in 847, he remained there until his death. Rabanus Maurus was above all a great master, so much so that he was subsequently given the title "Preceptor of Germany". Under his guidance the famous monastery of Fulda became the most prestigious cultural centre in Germany. Without taking part in political life, he approached the imperial power for the support necessary to his work in elevating the cultural and spiritual levels of the Germanic peoples. His literary works, always eminently practical in intention and encyclopedic in character, are in line with the demands of teaching and the apostolate. Many sacred hymns are attributed to him, among them the *Veni Creator Spiritus*. We give here an Easter hymn.

94. Let us sing in chorus, brothers, to the Lord our God,
his praises rising from souls, loving and devout,
while today we celebrate the Easter feast.
> Because Christ has risen from the tomb,
> let us be glad, in union with the choir of angels
> (refrain).

Once, indeed, the Lamb,
by the shedding of its blood,
led forth the Fathers from Egypt;
and now Christ himself, with his blood,
has ransomed us from the darkness of hell.

As Moses brought to safety
that great people across the Red sea,
while the enemy was brought to nothing,
so Christ has set us free by our baptism,
flooding the shore with the waters of his passion.

The Jews, in their frenzy,
decreed the death of Christ, the Master,
to be inflicted on him with the torments of the cross,
which, nor pious solicitudes,
nor the love of the Father for the Word,
were able to relieve.

Breathing out his soul, Christ entered the underworld;
triumphant, he banished the shadows of death,
the just he snatched away, the enemy he bound,
giving heaven to the good,
while evil men were left in their pains.

The stars of heaven,
the sea and all the earth, joy-filled,
sing their praise,
for Christ the Lord lives . . .

GREGORY OF NAREK

The period of the great cultural progress in Armenia, known as the first Armenian renaissance, and dating from the end of the 9th century, saw the emergence into the poetry of religion and liturgy of the mystic Gregory, a monk of the city of Narek. He lived from 951 to 1003 (or 1010) and in the silence of his monastery developed a natural capacity for listening and for loftiness. His lyrics are full of his anxiety over the social reality of the time and the suffering of the people living through it. His book of elegies, commonly called the *Narek*, can be considered as his masterpiece; he is also the author of panegyrics, odes and hymns. After the Bible, the *Narek* was the most read book in Armenia, because, in spite of the difficulty in penetrating into its full meaning, the people were able to discern in it something they already saw reflected in their soul.

95. With the seal of the cross,
     impressed with your blood,
     with which we have been baptized
     to make us ready for adoption,
     you have modelled us into the image of your glory.
     By all these divine gifts,
     Satan be put to confusion, his plots overturned,
     his snares evaded, the enemy vanquished,
     his sharp weapons repelled,
     light shine through the gloom,
     darkness be dispelled,
     mists fade away.
     Would that your arms might receive us
     into your protection,
     your right hand press its seal upon us.
     You are indeed full of love and clemency
     and your name is invoked over your faithful.
     To you, together with the Father,
     through the Holy Spirit,
     be glory and majesty through all ages. Amen.

96. O Sun of justice, blessed ray,
the first source of light;
O ardently Desired, above all else;
powerful, inscrutable, ineffable;
joy of the good, vision of fulfilled hope,
praised and heavenly, Christ the Creator;
king of glory, assurance of life,
fill the void of my miserable voice
with your almighty word;
and offer it as a supplication
pleasing to your Father Most High,
for you have come into the world in likeness to me,
subjecting yourself to human suffering,
the heritage of the curse.
O blessing of life, watchful providence
for all, both small and great!
If you accepted to die for me,
you, God and Lord of all,
how much more,
for the sake of the body you assumed, of your nature,
will you pardon the weakness that leads me into
    danger,
interceding for me, a sinner,
with the Father whose glory you share.

97. Good Lord, fountain of mercy,
giver of gifts, Son of the Most High, Jesus Christ:
have pity on me, rescue me, treat me with kindness,
help me in danger, heal the wounds of my heart.
Bend over my misery,
remove my doubts, and in the anguish that crushes me
come to the aid of the weakness that leads me astray.
Be as a doctor to me, in my sickness.
Listen with kindly ear to my pitiful moaning,
to the sigh that rises in silence from the abyss,
to the cry of my limbs reduced to dust . . .
I trust in you, Lord Jesus, listen to me,
you who alone are sovereign and almighty,

creator of heaven and of earth.
I await your coming
and hope firmly in your mercy.
I fall at your feet, kissing your footprints.
I confess my debts, acknowledging publicly my sins . . .
Graciously hear me, you who are full of bounty,
friend of men, forbearing, ineffably gentle,
day full of goodness and of endless light.
You alone can give to my soul,
even as it breathes its last,
salvation without end.
To you, with the Father and the Holy Spirit,
be glory for ever. Amen.

98. Eternal God, most kind and all powerful,
you who created light and made dark the night,
life in death and light in darkness,
hope for those who wait,
fortitude for those who doubt;
you who in your ever-active wisdom
turn into dawn the shadows of death;
Orient without decline, sun without setting;
night's darkness cannot veil
the glory of your power;
you, before whom will bend in adoration
the knee of every creature,
in heaven, on earth and in the underworld;
you who hear the groans of the prisoner,
listen to the prayer of the humble
and grant their request,
my God and my king, my life and my refuge,
my hope and my trust.
Christ Jesus, you, God of all,
the Holy One dwelling in the souls of the saints,
consolation of the afflicted
and propitiation for sinners;
you who know all things
even before they come into existence,

stretch forth the protecting right hand of your power
and free me from the attacks of darkness
and of the demon, so that,
ever kissing the vision of your holy and awesome face,
with the lips and desire of my soul,
I may live in safety
with those who invoke you with full hearts.

SIMON THE NEW THEOLOGIAN

Simon the New Theologian (c. 949–1022) is venerated as a saint by the dissident Orientals of the Byzantine rite and is known as a writer on mystical theology. Born at Galati in Paphlagonia, a region of Asiatic Turkey near the Black Sea, after an unsettled youth, he entered the Studion monastery at Constantinople. Ordained priest, he became superior of the monastery. After governing for 25 years he was deposed by the Sacred Synod on account of his excessive rigorism and sent into exile, from which he was recalled after one year. Simon preferred, however, to found a small monastery not far from Constantinople where he remained in retirement until his death. He was given the title of New Theologian, not for studies in speculative theology, but for his particular interpretation of mysticism. He wrote short treatises on ascetism, discourses and hymns from which we take the two given below.

99. It is you who are the kingdom of heaven, O Christ;
the earth promised to the humble of heart;
You are the meadow of paradise,
the supper room for the banquet divine;
You are the ineffable wedding hall,
the table that is laid for all;
You, the bread of life, the only real drink;
You, the fountain of water, and water of life;
You, the lamp that never burns low, given to your
   faithful;
You, the nuptial robe and royal crown;
You, the solace, the joy, the delight and the glory;
You, the happiness and the joyfulness;
and your grace, O God, will shine out like the sun;
grace of the spirit of holiness in all your saints;
and you, the inaccessible, will shine in their midst,
and all will receive light in the measure of their faith,
of their hope, of their charity and of their perfection,
of their purification and illumination;
O God, alone forbearing and judge of all.

100. O Christ, do not abandon me in the midst of this
world,
for I love you alone, even if as yet I have not known
you;
I look to you alone for strength to keep your
precepts;
I, who am completely in the power of my passions;
I, who do not know you;
would the one who has known you seek the pleasures
of the world?
Would the one who loves you search out other
pleasures?
Or feel the urge to seek another friend?
God, creator of the universe, giver of all that is
good in me,
in your kindness have compassion on my poor soul;
give me the gift of true discernment, that I may be
drawn
by the treasures of eternity and only those.
I will love you with my whole heart, seeking only
your glory,
not that which comes from man,
so that I may become entirely one with you
even now, and after death, thus attaining,
O Christ, to reign with you,
who for my sake accepted the most infamous of
deaths.
Then I will be the happiest among all men.
Amen, so be it, O Lord, now and for all ages.

INDEX

1. The hymnographers

2. Hymns arranged according to theme

The number is that given for the hymn in the text.

Hymns and prayers for Advent: 62, 63, 65, 66.

Hymns and prayers celebrating Christmas: 6, 22, 42, 62, 64, 77.

Epiphany hymn: 59.

Hymns and prayers exalting the mystery of the Passion: 32, 34, 57, 60, 72, 91, 92, 93.

Easter hymns: 10, 19, 22, 34, 35, 46, 73, 94.

Hymn for the Ascension: 29.

Penitential hymns and prayers: 12, 27, 28, 32, 39, 50, 53, 55, 74, 79, 81, 84, 85, 86, 87.

Morning hymns: 40, 41, 43, 58.

Evening hymns: 24, 36, 80.

Hymns to Christ:

— faith and love: 2, 3, 4, 13, 15, 28, 38, 75, 89, 99, 100.

— praise and gratitude: 5, 6, 7, 8, 11, 18, 23, 27, 31, 45, 47, 48, 51, 61, 67, 68, 69, 76, 86, 89.

— supplication: 6, 7, 11, 12, 14, 15, 25, 26, 30, 32, 35, 37, 44, 49, 50, 52, 55, 68, 71, 75, 76, 77, 78, 79, 81, 88, 90, 95, 96, 97, 98, 100.

Hymns with a reference to Mary, Mother of God: 18, 21, 22, 25, 27, 29, 31, 33, 34, 42, 48, 82, 85, 88, 91.